AT THE FLICK OF A COIN

MY EXPERIENCES AS A TEN POUND POM

from Bob

ENDORSEMENTS

'What a lovely chapters, I read it out to my husband and my voice broke a couple of times especially when you raised your hand and when you were quoting the George Beverly Shea words I'd rather have Jesus. So heart warming. I am sure the book is going to touch peoples lives when they read it.'

Veronica Nowell, Author: Ice Creams: A Trilogy

'I love the way God can take a person to the other side of the world with the purpose of introducing them to the Gospel of Jesus Christ. Such is the story of my friend Bob Oldershaw. The influence of New Zealand and Australia on his life was immense. The following chapters of this remarkable life hinged in him meeting and receiving Jesus to be his Lord and guide. A great read! A really special man. My friend, Bob Oldershaw.'

Reverend Canon Chris Bowater, OSL

Bob's book accurately provides detailed insight into how life was often difficult for migrants, particularly due to unsatisfactory accommodation upon arrival and the disparity from what was promised to that which was delivered.

James Yapp, Founder' Ten Pound Poms Facebook Group

'Bob has a fascinating way of writing his memoirs through his eyes as an eight year old child arriving in a different world to one he left behind in Maidenhead. As he starts telling his adventures as a newly arrived Ten Pound Pom it invokes memories of our first days down under as migrants. Snakes, mosquitoes, flies, spiders, brown rain water to drink and a strange lingo. But Bob survived and so did we. Who would live anywhere else but Australia?'

Peggy Hunt, Admin for Ten Pound Pom Facebook Group

AT THE FLICK OF A COIN

MY EXPERIENCES AS A TEN POUND POM

Bob Oldershaw

Publications

COPYRIGHT

DEDICATION

Firstly, to my Dad and Mum for having the courage to leave everything behind and start a new life in a country they had never seen and only heard about.

To Wendy, my wife, who said, "You must write a book about your experiences as a Ten Pound Pom. It will be great."
Well, here it is. Thank you Wendy, for your encouragement and putting up with me as I spent long hours on the computer over the last few months.

To my children, Daniel, Jonathan and Miriam. They have been an inspiration to me and a real blessing.

To my friends who have been a real support. Thank you.

CONTENTS

Foreword...ix

Introduction 1

Chapter One - On Board The Fairsky 3

Chapter Two - My Parents' Families 11

Chapter Three - My Family 23

Chapter Four - So What Was The Assisted Passage Scheme? 31

Chapter Five - The Ten Pound Lark 39

Chapter Six - Arriving In Brisbane 43

Chapter Seven - Moving On - Victoria Point 51

Chapter Eight - O'Halloran Point 59

Chapter Nine - Victoria Point State School 71

Chapter Ten - Corporal Punishment In Australia 85

Chapter Eleven - My Spiritual Search 89

Chapter Twelve - Link Road..93

Chapter Thirteen - New Zealand 109

Chapter Fourteen - Greenhithe...117

Chapter Fifteen - Problems At Home 125

Chapter Sixteen - Becoming A Christian In New Zealand............129

Chapter Seventeen - My Hitchhiking Adventure 139

Chapter Eighteen - Devonport..147

Chapter Nineteen - Leaving New Zealand 153

Chapter Twenty - Back In England.......................................157

Chapter Twenty-One - Any Regrets?......................................169

Appendix 1: Additional Photographs 179

Appendix 2: Photographical Information.................................189

Acknowledgements 195

References..197

About The Author 199

Index..201

Notes..205

Foreword

Australia, what does this word mean to you? What picture does it create in your mind?

Yes, it is impossible to think Australia without an image coming to mind, whether this is the Great Barrier Reef off the Queensland Coast, the jungles of the Blue Mountains in New South Wales or the vast expanses of desert. Australia has every climate you can imagine and amazing wildlife from great white sharks to koalas, kangaroos to redback spiders.

We have been warmed by the hospitality of its people from the Indigenous Australians to the descendants of those who were either deported or chose to travel to this incredible land.

We have enjoyed soap operas such as Neighbours, Home and Away, The Flying Doctors and McCleod's Daughters. We have watched celebrities scream 'Get me out of here!' and indulged in the warmth of cooking with Australian MasterChef's. TV programmes such as Skippy the Bush Kangaroo are ingrained in our DNA.

The chances are we have visited ourselves – as tourists, backpacking on crammed buses, trying to fit in as much as possible: the wildlife zoos to hold a baby emu and have a photo taken at an iconic location, such as Uluru or the Apostles on the Great Ocean road. If we haven't visited, we will know someone who has: a relative, a neighbor or even a postman.

We know so much about this country as it has been popularized in our culture in the past and continues to do so. Our King Charles is Australia's third Head of State, the yearly battle for the Ashes, and now Australia takes part in the Eurovision Song Contest. Plus, we embrace Australian celebrities, such as Kylie Minogue, Nicole Kidman, Hugh Jackman and Cate Blanchett among others who are ever popular in the UK.

Australia is familiar to us.

Although still considered long haul, you can travel to Australia in a reasonably short period of time. Leave today and you can arrive tomorrow. It is accessible but not so only a few years back. When migrants departed, it took several weeks on a ship. The promise made by recruiting officials did not always meet expectations.

The time Bob talks about in this book was long before the popularisation of culture had occurred. It was time of adventure, bravery and aspiration. It was uncommon for a family to decide to move to the other side of the world. Bob's family were as much pioneers as the original settlers of Australia.

Bob's parents made the decision to take advantage of government incentives to pay £10 and go and live work and raise families in Australia in 1961. He and his brothers had no choice. They would be one of thousands of families who took advantage of the Assisted Passage Migration Scheme.

It is hard to imagine the courage and effort required to uproot yourself and travel: the dreams of a better life, a different life, or something else. Bob remembers it vividly. Even though he remembers it from a child's eyes, the impact it has on his life, has made him an original character, formed his personality and informed his life choices.

Bob shares his vivid memories which take us through the full experience of being a Ten Pound Pom kid, travelling to Australia on board the Fairsky, living life in this new, exciting yet brutal land, we feel the pressure of trying to settle as a family and the pull of the Motherland, England, enticing them home.

At the Flick of a Coin is peppered with family photographs, an extract from his father's memoir and recollections from his brothers. I enjoyed a glimpse into the character of Bob's Mum, Dad, his brothers, Walter and Giles, and various friends. Bob's description of how they learnt their way in their new world, experimenting in ways youngsters today would never have the freedom to do.

We hear of the shenanigans Bob embroiled himself in, jumping off the quay or ferry (incurring the ferryman's displeasure), swimming in the shark-infested waters of the Pacific Ocean and creating toy soldier clubs. We hear of school life, in detail, which revealed Bob's creative writing side, even in the harshness of the times.

Even as a young child Bob was aware of his environment and difference between the Australia countryside and that of England. To a child it was easy to find happiness in nature despite the pressures of unhappy parental presence and an unstable father.

We travel with Bob as he moves from childhood, into adolescence and onto manhood and the spiritual awakening in him which gave Bob a deep faith to draw on. This faith must have helped with the unwanted move (from Bob's viewpoint) to New Zealand where Bob seriously put his life into God's hands.

My own family, my aunts and grandmother (on my father's side) also took up the £10 Assisted Passage Migration Scheme, leaving Glasgow to travel to Perth, but their recollections haven't been captured. Later, my Dad's siblings joined them and their children, grandchildren, and great grandchildren have made Australia their natural home.

So, I am grateful that Bob has chosen to tell his story and share what it was really like to be a Ten Pound Pom.

Ladey Adey,
Author - Unfrozen and Successful Business Networking Online

Introduction

I believe our most vivid and life impacting memories are those of our childhood.

I became a so-called 'Ten Pound Pom' in 1961, along with my two brothers and Mum and Dad. Australia had a big effect on my life growing up and formed (to a large extent) who I am today. I have many memories, which I will share with you, including the good, the bad and the ugly, starting from my memories as an eight year old. These memories are how I viewed life in Australia and from my own perspective. Other people who became Ten Pound Poms may have different views of what their lives were like at the time. The lifestyle in Australia I experienced in the 1960s is so far removed from present day life, I thought it would be interesting to share how we lived and coped in rural Australia; in the outback. In my book I refer to the Indigenous People as Aboriginals. It was the term used in those days. I will also be sharing a little about our dysfunctional family, my relationship with my father, mother and brothers. Why did my father flick a coin and decide to go to Australia, uprooting his family and leaving all his and his wife's relatives behind? Was he bored, frustrated, depressed and trying to escape his demons? Was he running away from something or running towards something - a better life maybe? I will also talk about my spiritual journey, which was very important to me (particularly as I was brought up in a non-religious household). My parents, as far as I knew, didn't have a particular faith, or at least none they shared with me, and in fact were very concerned when I became a Christian.

Although it took me a little while to get used to Australia and its people, I really grew very fond of it and would loved to have stayed after the five years we were there. In fact, I cried when I left and emigrated to New Zealand. I didn't want to leave, I wanted to stay and be with my friends, but it was not meant to be. I have a fairly positive outlook on life and try not to dwell on the 'what if's' and there were plenty of 'what ifs' and 'if only's' during the ten years we were in Australia and New Zealand. What if we had stayed in Australia? Life would have been very different for me. I had no choice in going to Australia when I was eight years old. When I was thirteen and we left Australia for New Zealand I still had no choice. Even when we left New Zealand I had no real choice in the matter, despite me being eighteen. I didn't have a job or anywhere to live. It would have been very difficult on my own.

Now, I live in England. I met my beautiful wife here and we have three wonderful children and now three grandchildren. What more could I want? I believe family and friends are the most important things in life. I found my true path in life with the help of my faith.

This is my journey.

Chapter One

ON BOARD THE FAIRSKY

I was very excited as I left home in Maidenhead. I said goodbye to my classmates and friends I had made in the neighbourhood. There was a lot of activity in our house in the weeks before we left: belongings were packed and our furniture sold. Relatives came round to say their goodbyes and we had to leave our beloved dog, Sappho, behind. I really missed him. Poor Sappho, I hoped he would be alright. So, the day came when we got in a taxi and went to Southampton docks.

I was eight years old when I climbed aboard the ship 'Fairsky', on the 2nd May 1961. This Italian Sitmar Liner took English people to Australia back in the 1960s and 1970s. Hundreds of thousands would travel as immigrants to Australia in this period of time. I was one of them. Although I didn't know it at the time, I was to become a 'Ten Pound Pom'. The journey took about five weeks, leaving Southampton and arriving in Brisbane at 7am on the 5th June 1961. There were 1,100 passengers on board.

My Mum and Dad, two brothers and I walked up the gangplank and stood on the deck of the ship with hundreds of others as we watched our relatives below on the dock side. There was lots of noise. Noise from the ship, blasting through the great big funnels. Noise from the crowds shouting their goodbyes, until they could no longer be heard. We had streamers which we threw to my aunts and uncles who saw us off, keeping hold of one end. Everyone was waving. Some, like Mum, were in tears as the boat slowly pulled out of harbour. I didn't know what all the fuss was about really. I saw this as an adventure and I was really excited. The streamers pulled tighter and tighter as the ship drifted out and then finally snapping. We continued to wave to our families and friends as we were moving away until they became tiny dots and we could no longer recognize them. Little did I know I wouldn't see them again for ten years.

It was exciting travelling on a big ship. We were free to roam around and explore. The cabin we slept in had bunk beds and I slept in the cramped cabin with Mum and my two brothers. We had some form of schooling for two hours in the morning and then we could do what we liked for the rest of the day. We swam in the ship's swimming pool which was fun. It was a great big square pool at the front of the ship where there was a set time for children to splash around in the salty water. Mum was happy to lie on a lounger and relax during the day.

Relaxing on the deck – Dad, Giles and Mum

Dad had a group of male friends he met up with for drinks, I'm not sure what Mum did for company. We were left running round the ship doing our own thing. We went for swims, played games, got in the way, watched films and generally had a good time and had decent meals.

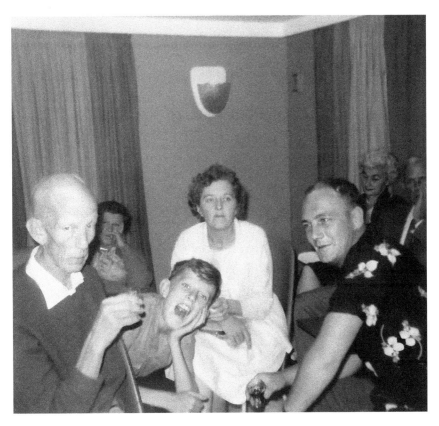

In one of the bars on ship; Dad, Walter and Mum with one of Dad's friends, Charlie

There was a cinema and we watched cartoons and some children's feature films. The food was marvellous and we had three cooked meals a day. For the first week, I was really sea sick and didn't feel much like eating. The best thing I could do was to lie down on my bunk bed for a while. It was a horrible feeling being sea sick and it's something I suffer from to this day. I could be sea sick in a dingy on a mill pond. After the first week, I was okay. It wasn't just me who was sea sick, most people were, especially when we were sailing around the Bay of Biscay which was particularly rough. The excitement of being on board was great. The ship was like one great big playground. It was a place to explore, running up and down the stairs, exploring the different decks and finding our way about. Mum and Dad weren't too concerned about us as it was not as if we were going to get lost.

My Dad wrote a narrative of what it was like for him on board ship. I'll share this later in the book. He was writing it for his friends, he called it, appropriately, 'The £10 Lark'. He wrote about his experience with the mates he met up with and who he spent most of the time with, Charlie, Joe and Spud. Walter and I would occasionally go into the bar to meet up with Dad and his friends.

Dad's new friends were going to New South Wales. No-one knew what they were going to do when they got there. We would see Charlie again in a few months after we had settled in Australia.

For a lot of the time the only thing we saw was the sea. As we sailed past the Bay of Biscay and headed into the Strait of Gibraltar the boat seemed to settle down and I felt alright. I believe this particular ship didn't have stabilisers which made it very rocky in rough weather. We travelled via the Mediterranean Sea and through the Suez Canal. The first stop was the Port of Aden where we were allowed to get off. Fortunately, the port was open at the time as Aden was under British Control, (a few years later there was a lot of resistance to the British and the port was closed for a time). Later on it would close again. We didn't stay too long in Aden, just a few hours as I recall.

Mum warned us not to drink the water as she thought it might be contaminated and to buy fizzy pop if we wanted a drink. We could get off the ship, which we did, and had a good look round the Port. It was very hot. Walter bought a wallet, which was genuine imitation leather. It was stolen as soon as he bought it (I think by the people who sold it to him). There were a lot of bargains to be had as goods were very cheap. Radios,

T.V. "FAIR SKY"   7.

QUEENSLAND   BRISBANE

NOMINAL ROLL OF ASSISTED PASSAGE MIGRANTS CONTINUED

```
                                                        :I the under-
                                                        :signed ack.
                                                        :to have re-
                                              :Amt. :ceived the
U.K. :                                        :(P.M):amount shown
REF. : NOM. :                  : DATE OF :    :Aust.:opposite
NO.  : REF. :    NAME          : BIRTH  :RLGN:OCCUPATION:Curr.:my name
                                                        £. s.

:QG350 :HAMMERSLEY                       :Elec.Welder:2.10::
        Thomas       :15. 9.1930:C.E.:(Safe-Trd.Flrg):(1/25):
        Joan         :28. 7.1933: "  :W         :      :
        Paul         :10. 4.1953: "  :C         :      :
        Michele      :21. 6.1956: "  :C         :      :
        Gary         :22.10.1957: "  :C         :      :
:QA13657:HILL                            :Sales Rep.:       :
        Alfred       :25.11.1921:C.E.:(Oil/petrol Dist):
        Sheila M.    :25. 1.1931: "  :W         :      :
        Elaine F.    :17. 9.1954: "  :C         :      :
        Nigel D.     :11.11.1955: "  :C         :      :
        Frances M.   : 9. 5.1958: "  :C         :      :
        Jocelyn M.   :21. 4.1960: "  :C         :      :

:QG350 :JOHNSTON                         :Bus       :2.10.:
        Bernard      :30. 1.1935:Cath:Conductor :(2/27):
        Rosemary G.  :28. 5.1937: "  :W         :      :
        Lynda A.     :26. 5.1956: "  :C         :      :
        Jacqueline T.:25. 6.1957: "  :C         :      :
        Denise G.    :22. 9.1958: "  :C         :      :
:QA13764:JONES                           :Fitter &  :
        Graham R.    :12. 1.1934:C.E.:Turner   : -  :
        Patricia     :19. 9.1934: "  :W         :      :
        Ann          :22. 3.1953: "  :C         :      :
        Peter R.     :29. 3.1958: "  :C         :      :

:QA13687:LAWSON (Miss)
        Jean A.      :11. 2.1931:C.E.:Typist    : -  :
:QG350  :LOWE                            :Motor Veh.:2.10.:
        Thomas E.    :16. 9.1930:Bapt:Driver/Intn:(2/7):
        Brenda       :23. 4.1930: "  :W         :      :
        John D.      : 8. 7.1954: "  :C         :      :

:QG350  :O'KANE                          :Proc.Wkr. :2.10.:
        Patrick J.   : 9. 4.1930:R.C.:(Chemicals):(2/27):
        Ethel R.     :14. 6.1927: "  :W         :      :
        Patricia J.  : 8.10.1952: "  :C         :      :
        Gary M.      : 7. 2.1954: "  :C         :      :
        Alan T.      :11. 8.1956: "  :C         :      :
        Antony G.    :23. 8.1957  " :C          :      :
:QA13695:OLDERSHAW
        Peter H.     :29.12.1904:C.E.:Clerk     : -  :
        Christabel J.:25.10.1918: "  :W         :      :
        Walter P.    :13. 4.1951: "  :C         :      :
        Robert E.    :16.12.1952: "  :C         :      :
        Giles L.     :27. 5.1954: "  :C         :      :

                    ASSISTED PASSAGES CONTINUED ......
```

Fairsky Nominal Roll of Passengers

binoculars, watches and so on were a lot cheaper than in England. The only problem was we couldn't afford anything.

It was a startling cultural experience for me. I had never seen dark skinned people before and it was fascinating to watch the Arab people shouting and bartering with the passengers on the ship. They were also allowed on the ship to barter their goods.

We weren't there long and we then proceeded with the long trip to Australia without stopping.

The journey from Aden to Australia was long with no stops. It took about four weeks and all we saw was the sea. I had got my sea legs by then and was making full use of everything we could do on the ship. It was May and the weather was turning warm, very different to the weather we had left in England. I got to see Mum and Dad at the meal times, but very little other than then. I would sometimes join Mum on the deck of the ship as she lay on a sun lounger; but Dad would be in the bar with his mates somewhere. I enjoyed the freedom to roam around and do what I wanted in relative safety.

Fairsky, Torrens ©

The first Australian stop was the city of Fremantle. This was a great big city and we were allowed to get off the ship and have a look around for a few hours. This was my first experience of Australia, and I really liked it. I liked the vast openness, the people, the friendliness and houses which didn't all look the same. I liked the city with its shops and hustle and bustle of people. As an eight year old, I couldn't really internalise how I felt but my first impressions would have a long and lasting impact on my life. It was slowly dawning in my young mind that there was a whole world out there to experience. A very different world to the one I left behind; in a council house on a suburban estate in Maidenhead with all houses looking the same.

Fremantle was the first city the migrants saw as they came to Australia. So, it became a flagship terminal: the authorities wanted to make a good impression as people got off the ship. There was a welcoming party to help people as they arrived. Fremantle had a lot of social significance and became a port of special importance.

Soon we were back on board and sailing again. We stopped off at various ports on the coast of Australia going from West to East. After travelling through the Great Australian Bight we reached Adelaide. I thought it was a great city. I can remember the long, straight roads running through the centre of the city. A large city, I was overwhelmed by its size. I had seen nothing like it.

Then it was onto Melbourne which took several more days. Many of the passengers disembarked to live there. I remembered Melbourne as a beautiful city, and I wouldn't have minded staying there. But it was not meant to be.

Our last but one stop was Sydney. Some more passengers got off here. There weren't many of us left on the ship. Finally (for us) we docked in Brisbane.

Chapter Two

MY PARENTS' FAMILIES

At this point, I would like to introduce my family, to give an understanding of what my mother and father and the rest of my family were like.

My father and mother were unusually matched. Dad was a very well-educated southerner and Mum was a northerner with secondary school education. He had been brought up with servants in a very large mansion called 'Fernley'. She was brought up as a working class girl in the backstreets of Blackpool in a three-bedroomed semi.

First Meeting

They first met after the war at an agricultural camp – a 'get-away from it all' farming camp, where the Government encouraged young people to go out and help the farmers. You were paid piecework - a system where you were paid based on your output and performance. Usually it earned enough to pay for your keep and perhaps a little bit for a glass or two of beer at the local. My mother met my father at one of these places. It was a very beautiful place, a manor house taken over during the war, and there were some German prisoners of war there too, working in the fields and

Mum and Dad in London, circa 1949 just after they got married

also cooking for the campers. Mum was a land girl and did odd jobs. Dad also worked on the farm, hay-bailing part of a working holiday for an ex-soldier who had seen active service in World War Two. Mum told me once that my Dad (Peter) picked her (Joyce) out for a dance once or twice. He was a good dancer but she didn't want any relationships at the time - she was getting away from it all herself and thinking hard about marrying someone else and going with him to America later on. He wasn't American but a Polish officer whose Jewish family had been carted off to the death camps. He, too, was intelligent, and spoke perfect English, read Chaucer, Shakespeare, Byron, and was educated in Switzerland. He was very kind and had a good sense of humour, but my mother had to think hard about it. Mum said she liked him a lot, but it wasn't love. She told him as kindly as she could so he could make a clean break after their two years of real friendship.

Two years later, she met my Dad again, by chance, at Charing Cross Station.

'Haven't we met before?' he asked in his rather slow, laconic style with a distinct Oxford accent. He was very tall, thin with an inscrutable expression. They had indeed met, at the farm two years earlier.

Mum, fourteen years younger than Peter, was hooked by his accent.

'Can I help you with your luggage?' he said in his Oxford drawl.

'Yes, thank you.' Mum replied in her broad northern accent.

He took her bags and off they went to another camp. The men were on one side and the women were on the other. They often worked on the same farm, but not always. They saw each other every night, at dances or walks to the local pub or wherever. Mum said Dad was difficult to get to know. Mum was very outspoken being a northerner, especially as a Lancashire girl. Sometimes he would get angry if she disagreed and sometimes he liked her getting annoyed. He was his own man and would never conform – to anyone. He would say the most outrageous things. For instance, there was a Mr Short on the farm. Dad would insist on calling him 'Shortarse' to annoy him, 'Shorty' always annoyed him too. Dad said Shorty was a horrid little man and wouldn't give you more than five minutes for a cup of tea and a break. Dad managed to ignore him most of the time, but 'Shorty' would often knock ten minutes off his pay for his name-calling. During this second camp, Dad asked Mum if she thought she could marry him. She said she might.

'Good', he said. 'Let's go and celebrate. I say, have you got any money? We'll have something at the pub. What would you like?' Mum would always end up paying.

They met for a further two years after camp and Dad would show my mother the Oxford College he studied at and they would go punting down the river. He gave her an engagement ring which actually fitted. It was a family ring, with a stag crest on it – similar to his own sapphire ring only a lady's. Unfortunately, later on it had to be pawned when they needed some money.

They married in the October of 1950. Dad was 46 years old and Mum was 32 years old.

Lucian – my grandfather

My grandfather, Lucian, went to Oxford University and gained an MA. He then started a private school at a large mansion called 'Fernley', which was a 'crammer' school to help students pass exams such as university entrance exams and conversion exams. Fernley was a large rambling mansion with a billiard room, squash courts and a tennis court. It was a little like a hotel where students stayed for a few weeks or even months. My father used to help out in the school by teaching Latin and Greek and various other subjects. Students came from all over the world and boarded there. As a school, Fernley collapsed financially after the war, as Lucian's partner set up a rival establishment.

Lucian, was married to Ethel Blogg. Ethel was the sister of Frances Blogg who married Gilbert Keith Chesterton, the famous author. So G. K. Chesterton (as he was known as, or just GKC) was my great uncle. Lucian introduced another famous author, Hilaire Belloc, to G. K. Chesterton. Due to my grandfather's influence and good standing (he was Mayor of Maidenhead twice) they got to know many famous people in the area. This contact with reknowned intellectuals had a profound effect on my Dad's attitude which was demonstrated in his arrogance throughout our later lives.

A lot of well-known and famous people came to visit the Oldershaws at Fernley. Stanley Spencer, the painter, was a regular visitor to my grandfather's house and became a family friend. One time my mother, who had not met Stanley before, answered the door and saw this rather bedraggled man at the door with a pram. (Stanley Spencer would always be seen pushing a pram which contained all his artist materials). She closed the door and went to tell Dad's mother Ethel, 'I think there's a tramp at the door wanting something.'

'Oh, that would be Stanley. Oh, do come in Stanley', Ethel said as she opened the door.

Another time, Ethel said to Stanley, 'Stanley, why can't you paint something nice? You can, you know.' Meaning she didn't like his very large nude drawings, but wanted him to paint some pretty pictures of houses and flowers.

Fernley, from the croquet lawn

In his younger days, my Dad often went to Lady Nancy Astor's house, Cliveden, and played tennis there.

My father had three sisters and a brother: Gertrude (known as Woozle), Pamela, Kate and Basil. They had had two nannies, Maude and Louie from when he was very young, so he was pampered from a very early age. When Dad was one and a half, Basil was born; when he was five and a half, Pam was born.

My Dad had a pact with his sister Pam. When they were in their teens they planned to commit suicide together. It was decided Pam would go first and then Dad. They were both going to jump from a veranda. Pam went first, as planned. Luckily, she didn't kill herself, but did injure herself very badly. Dad bottled out, fortunately for him. However, Pam never forgave him for the incident. His father, my grandfather, was so alarmed he had my dad sectioned for a time. I think my dad must have been mentally unbalanced. This took place before the war, probably in the early 1930's.

Family photo - Me Aunt Woozle, Mum, Dad, Giles and Walter

My dad had a lot of privileges when he was younger. He was sent to board at St Pauls' School for the finest education in the country, along with his brother Basil. Then he went on to Oxford University. He dropped out of Oxford after 1½ years as he couldn't (or wouldn't) take the pressure his father put him under. He was treated far better than his siblings though, apparently. At some point, he had a nervous breakdown and his mental health issues seemed to plague him all his life. He seemed a tormented soul at times. I could never find out why. Could it be because of the war and his war time experiences? He never discussed his time in the war and what he did, other than the information he was in the I-Corps, and involved in deciphering coded messages. I think this had a profound effect in his later life.

He was used to having servants when he was growing up in 'Fernley'. He helped his father in his tutoring business, teaching overseas students. There were quite a few servants and if he wanted anything he would just call one of them and they would do his bidding. In his later role as husband and father, he found the adjustment particularly difficult. He would from time to time revert back to his previous days and pretend Mum was a servant, which of course didn't go down too well.

Basil, unlike Dad, wasn't an academic. He had engineering leanings, and became an engineer for Rolls Royce.

Dad concentrated more on sports than he did on his studies. He also resented the fact his father got him a place at Oxford and he was following in his father's footsteps. My father was a bit of an enigma. A very highly educated man, who couldn't get a job. He was complicated and difficult to get to know. He also had a lot of resentment for certain members of his family for reasons only known to himself. Over the years he never quite got over this resentment, especially towards his father. His father, Lucian, had an affair with a younger woman for most of his married life which Ethel, his wife, knew about. I think Dad also resented his brother Basil for some reason. He got on well with his sister Kate though and much of the time, especially in Australia, he would ask Kate for money.

My Father sitting with the famous author G K Chesterton

My father was 48 when I was born but he looked a lot older. He felt more like a grandfather to me as I was growing up. My brothers and I had a reasonably good childhood. It was in the days of boys should be seen and not heard, so there was a lot of repressed emotions and being told off for things. We weren't allowed to express ourselves much, just expected to keep quiet, especially at the meal table. We usually ate in silence and would speak when spoken to. If we did talk we would be given a disapproving look. You had to behave 'correctly' at the meal table; eat with knife and fork, no elbows on the table and make sure everything was eaten, even if you didn't like it. It wasn't much fun really, but it was all we knew.

There's no doubt Dad was a very clever and intelligent man, but he was self-contained and self absorbed. He had some aspirations and would have liked to have been a writer. He didn't write any stories, but he did write a lot of poems. I think he felt overshadowed by his father and G. K. Chesterton and was probably a bit daunted by them.

Dad was closer to G. K. Chesterton than to his own father, Lucian. G. K. Chesterton loved children and, amongst other things, taught Dad and other children how to throw buns in the air and catch them with their mouths. Dad was about eight or nine when he first stayed with G. K. Chesterton and visited him many times over the years. In fact he was treated like the son they never had. Although Dad was a child, GKC never talked down to my father, but rather talked to him as if he were talking to an adult. In my father's late teenage years he would do some secretarial work for GKC.

My father was given a small inheritance in 1939 from the estate of G.K. Chesterton. It was the interest of the capital investment of £3000. It was enough to be able to manage living off the interest in those early years. Apparently, it would be the equivalent of about £168,000 in today's money. He couldn't touch the capital but would get the interest which amounted to several hundred pounds a year. Not much by today's standards but not too bad back then. Unfortunately, the interest was not compounded; my Dad took and spent all the interest every year and never re-invested and so the spending power went down and down, until over the years it was pretty much worthless. There was no way my parents could live off this alone. Sadly, Dad was used to a lifestyle of not having to work too hard and so ended up broke. Never in debt though, thank God, but never really enough for a comfortable lifestyle.

Jekyll and Hyde

My brother Giles thought Dad was a black and white character, a bit like Jekyll and Hyde. He said Dad didn't give people a second chance, and would quickly write them off if he didn't like them; and for the most part there seemed to be very few people he liked. It's not that he just didn't suffer fools gladly, he didn't suffer most people gladly.

Giles said Dad was like a closed book. He wouldn't let anyone into his private world. Consequently, no one really knew what he liked or disliked. He was very difficult to get to know. As a child, I so much wanted to get to know him but he wouldn't let me into his private world.

Giles thought Dad had a good time at Fernley and was used to lavish surroundings which made him feel he didn't need to have any ambition.

Dad seemed to be frightened of his own subconscious. He had no idea how to be in touch with other people. For some reason he couldn't bear people. He had many nightmares, very often persecuting dreams and had to be woken up from them. He looked on himself as a failure and was very sad about himself. He could be violent when we (children) were growing up. He couldn't hold down a job. Giles felt very sorry for him. I think I did too, although I didn't know how I could help him. Dad had asthma as a child which seemed to affect him as an adult and may have had a mental impact as well as a physical one.

Dad's Friends

Dad had a friend in England called Ronald Fuller, an author and critic, and was a contemporary of my Dad's at university: plus two or three he met on the ship coming out from England, Spud, Joe and Charlie. Dad had a wealth of literary knowledge but didn't really pursue it in terms of getting more qualified, bettering himself or advancing his career. Essentially, he was lazy. Giles said he initially followed Dad's way of living, becoming detached and relaxed to the point of irresponsibility. Giles had always liked Dad's interest in art but felt blocked for fear of possibly being seen as better or not able to follow in his footsteps.

My Mother and Her Family

My mother was born in 1918 in Blackpool to Nora and William Threlfall. She was one of three children, all girls and was the middle of the three. Greta was the oldest, then my mother, Joyce. Her first name was Christabel, but she preferred her second name, Joyce. Then Pam, the youngest of the three. They all really loved their parents and got on especially well with them.

Mum's Dad caught the flu back in 1918 and had health problems during his lifetime. The illnesses in those days were scarlet fever, whooping cough and tuberculosis. The big flu epidemic in 1918 was like the

Mum's family - Sisters, Greta and Pam, My Grandmother then Mum

plague. Mum's father got over it (when thousands didn't), but it left him deaf and with severe lung damage. He died aged 49. All the children had to communicate with him by sign language.

William was born to Jenny Threlfall and his father was Roderick Baines who came from an aristocratic background. They never married but had an affair. Roderick was upper class and would have been disinherited if he married beneath him. Jenny was the maid in the Baines' household. Roderick didn't have a huge amount of contact with either Jenny or William, he just saw them from time to time, but wrote loads of love letters to Jenny. Jenny had to bring up William on her own and with very little money. It was quite sad really as she and Roderick never got together in a relationship. It was all a bit long distance.

William married Nora and he got a job as a cabinet maker. They were very poor growing up. So the three girls had very little money, but all managed to get jobs. Greta was helped to go to university and get qualifications to teach. Pam also had a university education with financial assistance. Mum didn't get any assistance towards her education so she went out and got secretarial work. Although she got on well with her sisters, I think she felt left out and a bit hurt she wasn't given the opportunity to go to university like her sisters.

Chapter Three

MY FAMILY

My older brother Walter, was born in April 1951, I was born December 1952 and Giles, my younger brother, was born in May 1954. There was a year and a half apart between each of us. After Giles was born, my mother contracted tuberculosis and had to be hospitalised. There were no antibiotics in those days the only 'cure' was rest, recuperation and fresh air. She was hospitalised for nearly two years. In those days people who had tuberculosis were sent to a sanatorium for complete rest. This meant the patient had to lie in bed with no movement at all and preferably outside.

So we three children were sent out to various people but unfortunately not to the same people. I went to a hospital carer in Taplow, near Maidenhead. My only recollection of this time is I was looked after very well by a lovely caring nurse who really loved me. I would have been 1½ years old. Of course, I didn't know then I wouldn't see my mother for nearly two years. Giles went to a lady called Marjorie Brown and her husband, neighbours just a few doors away from where we lived. Mum handed baby Giles to her and said 'I'll be back soon, just going to the hospital'. Mum didn't realise how long she was going to be away for. Giles met up with them later on in his adult life. I think he was hoping to somehow reconnect with them but I don't think it really worked out and I think he was disappointed. I am not sure where Walter went to. I was told when Mum came to collect me after two years, I didn't recognise who she was. She was a complete stranger to me. I had been away from her from 1½ - 3½ years old (incredibly formative years). As I was led away by her, I screamed and screamed and screamed. In those days there was no gradual handover. It was like I was snatched away by a complete stranger. This was to be the first of many traumatic upheavals and departures in my life.

Me (left), Giles (centre) and Walter (right) with Mum

My relationship with both my parents was not always a comfortable one. Traumatised at an early age, my world was turned upside down almost from the start! Now we were all back together, all three brothers and my parents, but we were strangers. We were back together living in Maidenhead on a council estate: we lived together but we had no real bond.

My mother used to work but I don't remember where. One time we three children thought it would be a good idea to meet up with her and we walked a long way from our house. Unfortunately, she wasn't too pleased to see us as she then had to get off her bike and walk with us the rest of the way home. Ah well. We brothers used to go off together by ourselves quite a lot.

We used to go the nearby dump and try to find things. Once my brother brought back a piece of marble which I thought was great. I got a bit jealous and I prayed I would find a bigger piece. Within seconds I had found a slab of marble which must have been about five feet long, too big for me even to carry. It was the first prayer I had prayed and one which was answered immediately. I wasn't brought up to pray or believe in God or anything. It would be the start of a spiritual journey for me.

One time my older brother saw a bees nest and threw a stone at it. It was deliberate on his part as he wanted the bees to get angry and attack me, which unfortunately they did. It was just one of the many things Walter did to wind me up. The council estate was pretty rough where we lived, I remember getting tied to a tree and being left there for hours to be collected later by my father. As I said, my parents didn't seem overly bothered about our movements or what we got up to. It really was a different era, and most families were the same, where you would leave your kids for hours outside just doing their own thing. My brother Giles remembers an incident where we went to Maidenhead which was just under two miles from where we lived and my mother just left us in a park to play while she went off to do some shopping. It seemed the normal thing to do with some families. Giles recalls we were picked up by a couple who took us to their house where we stayed for a few hours. Eventually my mother came to get us. She had no idea where we were but the couple must have looked out for her and we were reunited. I would have been about six and Giles about five at the time. In those days children used to play outside all the time with no restrictions and no adults supervising them, not like today. It seemed like a much safer society in those days.

Walter was always experimenting with things. He had burnt a rubber tyre in the back garden for some reason. My parents obviously didn't spot him doing it. Some of the burning rubber fell onto his knee which must have been incredibly painful. He still bears the scar to this day. His experiments usually involved me. When I was just a baby, Walter thought it would be a good idea to stuff a plastic ball down my throat. It got stuck and I was choking and turning blue. My mother whisked me out of the pram and ran to the nearest hospital holding me upside down. Thankfully I survived!

We used to play with other kids off the estate. Some of the kids were good and others were not so good. We went to a quarry with a large pool of water at the bottom. I was at the top of a small hill leading into the quarry and my mate challenged me to push a little kid in to the water. So I ran down the hill and pushed him in. I didn't realise the consequences, I was only about five. He lost his shoe in the process, got soaking wet and cried a lot. I felt terrible. I came back later to try and find his shoe but couldn't.

We had lots of visitors from our many relatives. I didn't really know them all but there was one really nice man called 'Tom' (Ernest Oldershaw) we called him Uncle Tom and he was my godfather, although he didn't really do all required of a godfather, but when he did come and see us he always brought sweets and we played with his funny walking stick. It was a stick which could grab things.

Aunt Woozle would often come round to see us too, when we were in England. Sadly, she liked to drink a lot as did her husband.

I don't think I was particularly happy as a child, my parents weren't happy either and their dissatisfaction with life seemed to rub off on us. They didn't relate to us very well and so I never really had any meaningful conversations with either of them, but I believed they loved us although it wasn't always apparent.

Even my brothers and I were rather disparate. It could have been because we didn't really know each other until we all came out of foster care. Giles and Walter got on well together and used to enjoy each other's company. Being a middle child I was kind of betwixt and between. We all got on but

I had other interests and used to pursue them. Giles and Walter would do things together and I would find myself alone. I think it had a lot to do with us being separated when Mum went into hospital.

My early schooling

I found schooling difficult and unenjoyable. My school was Larchfield Primary School. My older brother and I were nearly always late and we would always have to go to the headmaster's office. My brother would get a table tennis bat on the backside and I would be let off for some reason - perhaps because I was younger, about seven. The headmaster couldn't

Me by the River Thames, with our beloved dog, Sappho.

get his head round the fact it perhaps wasn't our fault we were always late, but he wasn't interested in excuses. I can't remember learning anything at school. My younger brother went to a different school and he always fell asleep, so he never learnt anything. As for me, I was once asked to write out the twelve times table as a punishment. I had no idea what the headmaster was asking me to do so I rough scribbled some rubbish on a bit of paper and gave it to him. He looked at it in horror but didn't really say anything. I think he must have known he was asking me to do something I had never been taught. I enjoyed school though and got on well with the other children in my class and would later write to them all when we eventually touched down in Australia.

Life in England at the time was bleak as the war had not long finished. There was lots of repair work being done to buildings. I remember going into Maidenhead and seeing some demolished buildings with rubble everywhere. People were optimistic now the war had finished but everything seemed so grey and colourless. Perhaps this is what drove my parents to choose to go to Australia. This and the thought of another bleak and cold winter.

We were very poor, needless to say, and we went to school in very tatty clothes. One occasion when we were going to have injections on our bottoms I knew I would have to take my shorts down and reveal my raggy underpants, so I decided not to wear them and get embarrassed. I think I was even more embarrassed when the nurse told me to take down my pants and I had to reveal I was not wearing any underpants. This was just one of many embarrassing episodes in my early life.

I often had my own bedroom, I don't know why, but Walter and Giles shared a bedroom. Mum would come into my room when I settled down to sleep and she would sing me songs or tell me a story. She would sing with such emotion, even now the songs I love to hear are the ones which move me to tears and stir my soul.

One of the songs she regularly sang to me was 'Bobby Shaftoe'.

> Bobby Shaftoe's gone to sea,
> With silver buckles on his knee;
> He'll come back and marry me,
> Bonny Bobby Shaftoe.
>
> Bobby Shaftoe's bright and fair,
> Combing down his yellow hair,
> He's ma ain for ever mair,
> Bonny Bobby Shaftoe

It was particularly poignant as she always called me Bobby. In fact it was only Mum and Dad who would call me Bobby and sometimes it seemed there was a special bond between my mother and me. She understood me and seemed to know what I was thinking. Maybe it was because I was the middle child with a middle child syndrome. Perhaps she felt I was somehow missing out, with both Walter and Giles getting more attention and me being sandwiched in the middle. I certainly did feel at times unable to relate fully with either Giles or Walter. It is why I mostly did 'my own thing' and have been fiercely independent for most of my life. Even though Mum tried to compensate for my feelings of loneliness and isolation I still had these feelings throughout my early life.

She used to read stories 'out of her head' as we used to say to her. I didn't want a story from a book, it had to be out of her head. She made up some remarkable stories, all about Rupert Bear. In fact, I still have a Rupert Bear from my childhood days.

Molly Malone is another song she used to sing to me when she was putting me to bed,

> "Molly Malone"
> In Dublin's fair city
> Where the girls are so pretty
> I first set my eyes on sweet Molly Malone

As she wheeled her wheel-barrow
Through streets broad and narrow
Crying, "Cockles and mussels, alive, alive, oh"

"Alive, alive, oh
Alive, alive, oh"
Crying "Cockles and mussels, alive, alive, oh"

Chapter Four

SO WHAT WAS THE ASSISTED PASSAGE SCHEME?

Ten Pound Poms (or Ten Pound Tourists) was a colloquial term used in Australia and New Zealand to describe British citizens who migrated to Australia and New Zealand after the Second World War. The Government of Australia initiated the Assisted Passage Migration Scheme in 1945, and the Government of New Zealand initiated a similar scheme in July 1947. Ten Pound Poms were called this because they only had to pay £10 in processing fees to migrate to Australia, and the Commonwealth arranged for assisted passage on chartered ships and aircraft. Children could travel for free. Of course, because of the cheap fare a lot of Britons took advantage of this scheme and thousands emigrated.

The Assisted Passage Migration Scheme was created in 1945 by the Chifley Government in Australia and its first Minister for Immigration, Arthur Calwell, as part of the "Populate or Perish" policy. It was intended to substantially increase the population of Australia and to supply workers for the country's booming industries.

In return for subsidising the cost of travelling to Australia, adult migrants were charged only ten pounds for the fare and child migrants travelled free of charge. The Government promised employment prospects, affordable housing and a generally more optimistic lifestyle. It was a glamorous sales pitch which often didn't match up to the reality. On arrival, migrants were placed in basic hostels and the expected job opportunities were not always readily available. More often than not, the migrants were stuck in the hostels for weeks at a time, sometimes months and even years.

The scheme followed the so called 'Big Brother Movement' and attracted over one million migrants from the British Isles between 1945 and 1972. This was to be the last substantial scheme for migration from the British Isles to Australia. However, in recent years there has been a trawl for British workers to emigrate to Australia and at the time of writing there has been another trawl for nearly 30,000 people to fill gaps in certain key sectors of industry particularly in Western Australia.

In 1957, more migrants were encouraged to travel following a campaign called 'Bring out a Briton'. During this year, over 80,000 migrants took advantage of the scheme. The scheme reached its peak in 1969 and finally came to an end in 1982.

The Fairsky's History

As I mentioned, we went to Australia on the Fairsky. This was one of many ships which carried immigrants to Australia. Other ships include the Fairsea and Castel Felice. These ships were Italian liners. The Fairsky started life as a cargo ship in 1941 and was named 'Steel Artisan'. At the start of the Second World War the US government took it over and it became an aircraft carrier. It was soon taken over by the Navy as an assault carrier and renamed HMS Attacker. Attacker saw extensive wartime service as an assault carrier for the remainder of the war. In September 1945, HMS Attacker was present at Singapore as part of the allied force. It was used for reoccupation, sailing immediately afterwards for the Clyde to de-store and enter reserve. So, the vessel had seen quite a bit of history already!

The vessel was returned to the custody of the United States Navy at Norfolk, Virginia in December 1945 and was struck from the U.S. Navy list in February 1946. The ship was next sold to the U.S. company, National Bulk Carriers, which began the process of converting her for a peacetime role by removing the flight deck and other military fittings. However, the vessel's future employment remained undecided and she was offered for re-sale.

Conversion to Ocean Liner

In 1950, before The Fairsky was converted to Ocean Liner she was temporarily named Castel Forte and was intended to be a refrigerated cargo ship. However, this conversion was soon abandoned and the vessel returned to lay-up. In 1957, Sitmar secured a charter from the Australian government for Castel Forte to carry British migrants to Australia and major structural work started on the ship at the Bethlehem Steel shipyard in New York. The vessel was moved to Genoa in December 1957, where the interior refitting was completed in May 1958. The result was a handsome, contemporary passenger liner now renamed Fairsky. Tourist One Class accommodation for a maximum of 1,461 was provided in 461 cabins over five decks. Reflecting similar arrangements in earlier company ships, Fairsea and Castel Felice, Fairsky featured just seven cabins with private facilities, located forward on the Sun Deck, beneath the Bridge Deck. Air-conditioning was installed throughout the ship and a good range of comfortable public rooms were provided, mostly on the Boat Deck. At the back of the ship (aft) on this deck, an attractive lido area including swimming pool (built over the top of a deep hold hatch) was also situated. This is where we spent most days in the salty water. It was primitive compared to what is available now on ocean liners, but we didn't know any different back then and thought it was great fun.

Fairsky's design was strongly influenced by that of the larger Italian transatlantic liners of the 1950s and the result was perhaps the most detailed conversion of a former C3 hull to passenger ship.

Fairsky joined the Fairsea and Castel Felice (originally the British-India Steam Navigation Company's Kenya of 1931), plying the migrant route between Europe and Australia. Sitmar had become the first non-British company to secure a contract to carry British migrants. While a familiar sight in Australian ports since 1949, the latterly upgraded Fairsea operated the first voyage under this particular charter, departing Southampton on 6th December 1955 and arriving at Sydney on 12th January 1956.

While precise figures are not available, the four ships were responsible for the transportation of hundreds of thousands of European settlers to Australia, spanning over 20 years in total. Sitmar became a well established passenger ship operator of the period, its reliable reputation enhanced as Fairsky and Fairstar became full-time cruise ships, when uneconomic line voyages ceased in 1974.

Life on board

The journey to Australia usually took about five weeks when going through the Suez Canal. There was another route the ships took when the Suez Canal was blocked and went past the West Coast of Africa. This would be a lot longer trip than going through the Suez Canal, but it would have been more interesting. The ship would stop off at Las Palmas in Grand Canaria, one of the Canary Islands, where you could get off and have a look around at this beautiful island. The next stop would be Cape Town. Again, you could get off and go up to Table Mountain or just look around the local area. The ship had to provide various activities for the passengers, to keep them amused and entertained on this long and often boring voyage when all they saw for most of the journey was the open sea. The passengers were encouraged to form a sports committee to play deck games and tournaments. I remember playing quoits on one of the decks. However, as children, we were also entertained by some of the

At sea. Me (on left) with Giles.

crew with various children's activities.

Fairsky was designed for long voyages, with five open, teak-clad upper decks including a deep swimming pool aft, courts marked for deck tennis and quoits, also ping-pong tables which were popular with all age groups. The ship featured three dining rooms and there were two sittings. A full menu was provided for each sitting and you could have what you liked from the menu. The children ate separately from their parents for some reason. There was a grand social hall, children's playroom, a writing room and library, Bavarian tavern, two further bars and a cinema. My father enjoyed spending his time in the bars and the alcohol was very cheap, just 10p for a shot of whisky.

Medical facilities included a fully equipped hospital with operating theatre and isolation ward.

On deck (right) with my brother, Giles - ready to play a game of bowls on deck.

Fairsky's staff provided frequent entertainment for the passengers, details of which were widely displayed throughout the ship on the daily activities program. Dinner dances and variety shows were periodically staged. One of the guest bands who played on the ships was The Seekers on their way to the UK to begin a career which would bring their music into homes all over the world - they weren't on our ship though. Other events included the obligatory mock ceremony (performed by the ship's Italian crew, with the help of passenger 'volunteers') when the vessel crossed the equator.

Fairsky's own popular musicians usually played requests in the public rooms before dinner, also in the dining rooms on gala nights such as the Captain's welcome and farewell and 'fancy dress' theme evenings. Travelogues and recently released films were screened daily in the dedicated cinema. Children were also thoughtfully catered for with their own meal sittings at lunch and tea times, entertainment shows, cartoon screenings and occasional lessons provided, usually about the history of Australia. At the end of the voyage, each child would also receive, at random, a quality toy provided by the Line free of charge.

Typical highlights of the voyage included the trip through the Suez Canal, where local youths in 'bum boats' dived for coins thrown by passengers, and the stop at the Yemeni Port of Aden – the only time on the voyage where passengers had the opportunity to leave the ship and stretch their legs. Aden was also a place where passengers could pick up cheap consumer goods from around the world, or products made by the local tourist industry such as rag dolls stuffed with sand or leather wallets with ancient Egyptian motifs. More intrepid passengers could take a taxi trip out of the city to surrounding villages, where they were likely to be mobbed by crowds of poor children begging for money.

Following the call at Aden, the journey would often resume as a long uninterrupted voyage to Australia. The ship would first berth at Fremantle, Western Australia, then steam through the Great Australian Bight to Melbourne, Victoria and finally onto Sydney, New South Wales, dropping passengers off at each point. The voyage through the typically rough seas of the Bight would not uncommonly add a high point of excitement for the children on board and a low point – through seasickness – for the adults. Additional stops would sometimes be made at Adelaide in South Australia, Brisbane in Queensland and on to Auckland in in New Zealand. Our stop would be in Brisbane.

A certificate given to everyone when the ship crossed the equator - 18th May 1961

Chapter Five

THE TEN POUND LARK

My father kept a journal of life on board the Fairsky. The following is my father's memoir of what life on board was like and his experiences. He was friends with three other men who were his cabin mates on board, Charlie, Spud and Joe. He called this memoir, appropriately, '*The Ten Pound Lark*'. Here is some of what he wrote.

> *"'Hallo! Are you on this Lark?*
> *"Yes; good idea isn't it? I'm Charlie; this is Joe; this is Spud. What's your name?"*
>
> *I replied and introduced myself to the group. I got on well with them throughout the voyage. Surprisingly, as they were all very different with diverse backgrounds.*
>
> *Charlie had come from Southport; Spud from Belfast; Joe from some part of London. Charlie had been in the Merchant Navy; Spud on the Dole. Joe did not commit himself. I rather proudly said that I had worked in the Passport Office.*
>
> *'Charlie's conversation consisted mostly of chaff. Spud's consisted entirely of giggles and obscenities; Joe, when he spoke at all, spoke with slow deliberation. He had a slightly Chinese face and an air of mystery. He said he thought he would be all right in Sydney as big*

cities were much the same all over the world, and he knew his way about them. He would be no good in the Bush. Charlie said he was going to try beachcombing; Spud said he was going to stay on the Dole, if possible. He wondered if he could continue to draw it on the boat. I said I would share a portion of the beach with Charlie.

All I knew of Australia was derived from the novels of Neville Shute; a brief passage in Stevenson's The Wrecker, and a tale I had once read in a Boys' magazine about a man escaping from a penal settlement. There was also, of course, the final chapter of David Copperfield, suggesting, as Chesterton pointed out, that it is a kind of 'Island Paradise', attached to England, where the souls of the socially dead are ferried across to live in Everlasting Bliss. Stevenson's few pages about the remittance man seemed the most realistic on the whole. No other author I had read seemed ever to have touched on it, except in mockery; and it may be that Belloc's derisive exhortation to the lachrymose Lord Lundy still expressed the popular attitude; 'Go out and govern New South Wales!'

Charlie, who slept in the bunk above mine, asked me to account for my movements during the evening. I said I had been ministering to my wife, who was sea-sick, and had then made a tour of the ship. Did he want a full itinerary? He laughed and began to talk about the night's festivities: how he had begun with beers and brandies and ended up with 'Pyjama Man' and another called 'Cowboy', who had to be carried to his cabin. Pyjama Man was nasty and Cowboy silly. Spud giggled and Joe laughed in a sociable way.

Later, Charlie asked me to recite some poetry,

"Yes, do," repeated Spud to my surprise.

I recited some lines of Housman which seemed appropriate: "Could man be drunk forever." They approved of this and said it was very true, but Charlie wished I could remember "Horatius" from which he misquoted a line in a voice charged with alcoholic emotion. But Horatius was a friend of my boyhood whom I did not wish to meet again in the present circumstances. His reappearance embarrassed me as much as his appearance embarrassed Lars Porsena and co. I wanted to be left to my meditations. I had packed in a hurry with a thousand things left undone, but what weighed most heavily on my conscience was my desertions of Sappho the near Spaniel, who, after being escorted to a dozen prospective homes had always returned triumphantly on the doorstep to the only possible one for her. She remained to the last and crouched beside me in the car to Waterloo. I did not care to think of her present predicament, but continued to do so nevertheless. After all, one could not have one's destiny controlled by a dog (bitch), or could one? Journeys had been abandoned for more trivial reasons: for some anomaly in the structure of a goat.

"Good night all," said Charlie.

"I think we ought to have a drink sometime." I said to Charlie the following morning. "Charlie readily agreed.

"I'll be at the Bavarian Bar from 7 onwards", he said. "Meet me there and we'll join The Boys."

"I'll do my best," I said. "It depends on my domestic duties."

But as it happened it worked out all right. I was passing through and there was Charlie standing by the Bar. I was a little dubious all the same. What about this £10 Lark? Who had the money?

"Hallo, Charlie! What are you drinking?"

"No. This is on me. Put your money away, Peter."

"No. I asked you to have a drink."

"I'll have a lager then."

"Two lagers, please."

"English or Australian?"

"Any Dutch?"

"No, no Dutch."

"All right: Australian. We'll have to drink it sometime."

Very good, we agreed.

"What's yours, Peter? I'm having a brandy."

"Thank you."

We were suddenly surrounded by The Boys, that is, all except 'Soho' Joe, who, they said had 'fallen out'. It was suggested I should take his place. Spud was leaning over me, giggling away. Charlie introduced me to Jack, who looked like a prize fighter. He asked me where I thought he came from. I said probably from Ireland. But he said he came from Poland, though his mother was Irish. I meditated upon this matter as another round of brandies appeared. It seemed to be of absorbing interest. I looked towards the steward to see if he was in the secret of the £10 Lark, but he kept renewing the brandies with practiced, automatic gestures.

"Once in a lifetime", said Charlie, "only a shilling a glass. Might as well make the most of it."

"The boat seems to be rocking a bit." I said. "I thought we had cleared the Bay of Biscay."

Chapter Six

ARRIVING IN BRISBANE

Our final port was Brisbane, where we were going to get off the ship. Out of over 1000 passengers on board at the start of the voyage there were only about 80 left, all getting off at Brisbane. Presumably the ship was heading off back to England ready to pick up more passengers and take them to Australia. This was the last stop and we had to get off there. I found out later my parents had no option but to get off.

We arrived in June which is the Australian winter. We needn't have worried about the weather as it was quite warm. We had to stay in an immigration centre, which as I remember was pretty grim. It was a big immigration centre for all the migrants from England and other countries. We had to be registered and found accommodation. This was a real culture shock especially after all the glossy adverts about living the life down under, advertising it in a rather idyllic, romanticised way. It seemed at the time it couldn't be further from the truth.

Transit accommodation in general was basic and usually Nissan huts. I think the accommodation was deliberately bad to deter immigrants overstaying their welcome. They would hopefully want the adults to get out and look for jobs and accommodation sooner rather than later. I believe some immigrants returned back to the UK within days of staying there as they found the culture shock was too great. It was not what we were expecting. Fortunately, my parents stuck it out and we we were not there for long, just a few weeks until my parents found work and somewhere to live. I don't remember too much about those early days except I was glad to get out and into a normal house.

Brisbane

This is where we would be living for the next few weeks at least. It was primitive, and was full of English families and other nationalities all coming to Australia to seek a better life. It was here I first heard the term Pommie. I didn't know what it meant, but it felt like a derogatory word at the time. I was later to learn Pommie was a term used for English immigrants. It was supposedly an acronym for Prisoners of Mother England or Prisoners of Her Majesties Empire although this is not substantiated. There seems to be a lot of confusion about the origins of the word. More likely the word 'pommie' or 'pommy' derives from pomegranate because of its red or ruddy complexion, much like the English complexion apparently. The English were also called Limeys because they ate limes to ward off scurvy on the long sea voyage. The word pomegranate probably sounded like Pommy grant which could be

A typical transit camp of Nissan Huts where migrants would be housed.

a rhyming slang for immigrant. This term was used well before the First World War. Well, whatever the derivation it wasn't a term of endearment and the phrase, 'Go home you Pommies' and other such phrases were commonly used by the locals.

There were many transit camps which provided temporary accommodation for immigrants, these included; Wacol Hostel, Stuart Camp, Yungaba Immigration Centre and the Comslie Immigration Centre. We stayed at the Yungaba Immigration Centre and we were there for about ten days. We didn't particularly enjoy our stay there. It was very spartan, the food and facilities very basic. It was, however, better than some of the transit accommodation offered to many immigrants. Yungaba had an interesting history. It was designed and built in 1885 as an immigration centre and housed its first immigrants in 1887. Over the years, it housed inmates from an asylum, South Sea Islanders and was converted to a hospital during both World Wars. It then became a proper immigration centre housing a limited number of migrants. The volume of post-war immigration was immense and as such, the hostel was unable to cope with more than a small proportion of new arrivals. The bulk of the immigrants were redirected to the many empty military camps around the city. Of these, Camp Columbia at Wacol was

Yungaba Immigration Centre Main Building

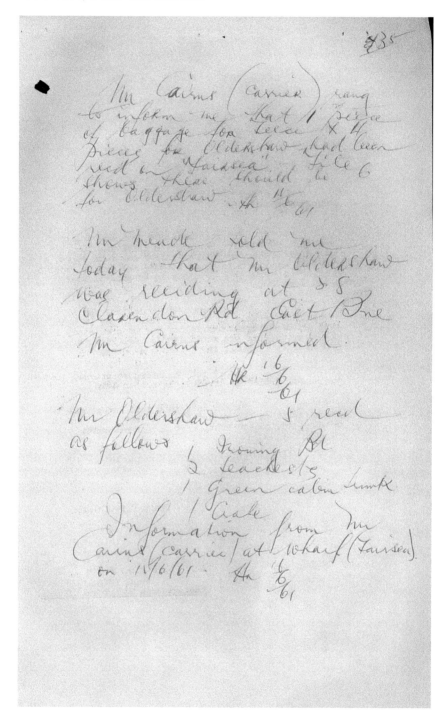

Fairsky manifest stating luggage for Oldershaws on the Fairsea

perhaps the best known. The name 'Yungaba' derives from the Gubbi Gubbi Aboriginal language from the Maroochy area and means 'place of sunshine'.

East Brisbane

After ten days we moved to Clarendon Street, East Brisbane. Life suddenly became a lot better and the shock of arrival in a foreign land was more tolerable. We had to wait for our boxes and suitcases to arrive however, which were on another ship, TSS Fairstar. Fortunately, they arrived in the next few days.

The house we rented was a fairly new, lovely house with modern furniture. Much better than the council house we left behind in England. The council house where we didn't have a bed but slept on mattresses on the floor and all of us three children in the one room. The council estate where every home was the same and the houses were all crammed together in a tiny space. This new house had bunk beds and there was a proper table and chairs. We really settled down in our new environment. I even had a bike. It didn't have any gears on it or anything like: it was pretty basic. I rode around with some of the local kids. One time as we were on our bikes riding around the estate with them I said 'Tally Ho' in my posh English accent as we were riding along. It just came out quite naturally. They found this quaint English saying quite amusing. In fact, we got on well with our neighbours. They seemed to like us 'poms'. Life was pretty good for a while. Our experience later on in Australia was to be very different.

The house, the neighbourhood and Brisbane itself was a world away from where we lived in England and our lifestyle there. Much, much better in every way. We quickly got settled in a new school, the East Brisbane State School. We stayed there a few weeks and Mum got a job. But Dad didn't.

I wasn't sure how long we would be staying there in East Brisbane. I wasn't in on the plan about what we were doing or where we were going to live or which school we would be going to. I'm sure my parents had a plan but I wasn't told.

Everything was new to me. The people spoke with a different accent and at times difficult to understand. 'G'day', 'Yer right' and 'fair dinkum' were common phrases. Phrases I would have to learn if I was to integrate with the Australians. Also, if the Aussies could say what they wanted to say with the least amount of words they would. For example, 'Are you going down to the beach this afternoon?' would be translated 'Goin' down the beach s'arvo?' 'She's a beaut' – usually referring to a car as in 'that car is really beautiful', or 'fair dinkum sport' meaning 'that's really true my friend.' I'm sure my Australian friends found my accent a bit difficult to understand as well, but I gradually acquired some sort of Australian accent.

EAST BRISBANE SCHOOL

Our first school in Australia was the East Brisbane State School. My two brothers and I really enjoyed this school and the teachers were kind. I got on well with the other children in the class who seemed genuinely interested in these strange, very white, English people. This was very different to the school in England where we used to get whacked most days for being late, which didn't put us in a good frame of mind for learning anything. Here, the teachers were very supportive and helpful. I learned a lot in the short few weeks I was there. Walter liked one of his lady teachers so much, he kissed her. I'm sure she appreciated it! Things were looking good. We had to buy a whole lot of books and carry them in a strange bag called a 'port', short for the word 'portmanteau'. It was like a leather satchel which you carried on your back with all your books and lunch in.

My mother applied for a job at a local Golf club in East Brisbane as a secretary. There was a long line of people all wanting the same job. It seemed Mum was in the queue for hours, waiting for an interview. The manager got frustrated and bored as he interviewed so many people. The hours ticked by and the queue got shorter. Then it was my mother's turn to be interviewed. When she said who she was and what she did, that she had previously worked as a secretary in England he immediately said to those in the long queue, 'Right everybody, you can all go home now. I have found the person I want.' Mum got the job. She felt a bit embarrassed and sorry for the others as they had been queueing for hours. She could start work straight away. She very much enjoyed the work and it looked like we were settled at last. Unfortunately, Dad didn't (or couldn't) get a job. It was so difficult to get a job in those days especially for older people. Who wants a 57 year old man with no qualifications? My father also looked a lot older than his years and often looked like a man in his 70s. So, he was not able to find any work. My parents couldn't really manage on just Mum's wage and this was the reason we left our beautiful home in East Brisbane. We were also to leave our school we liked so much. Of course, I didn't understand the reasons for leaving at the time.

We were on the move again. As usual, we children didn't know where we were going or what was happening. Maybe we didn't need to know.

Chapter Seven

MOVING ON - VICTORIA POINT

The removal van came in the morning and collected our belongings, such as they were. The rest of our stuff, which had been stored in the hold of the ship, was still awaiting delivery at some future time. They were in several tea chests which we later used as tables when they were finally delivered. The three of us boys were loaded in to the back of the windowless furniture removals van. We drove to our next destination. Mum and Dad were in the cab with the driver. We had no idea how long the journey would take as we sat uncomfortably on the floor in the back of the pitch black van. The journey probably took about an hour to Victoria Point but it seemed a lot longer. Victoria Point in Queensland is on the East coast about 22 miles away from Brisbane.

We arrived at our new house in Victoria Point. Victoria Point was very rural in those days. There weren't many houses. The house was split into two flats. The owners lived in one part and we had the other, which had two bedrooms for the five of us. We kids were glad to explore our new surroundings. It was very different to the very urban area we had just came from.

We were on the coast just minutes away from the sea. There was even an island, called Coochiemudlo, which we could get to by ferry. It was July and the temperature was still nice and warm even though it was the middle of winter. There were three shops in the small village. One of the shops, owned by our landlady, sold all the basic groceries. I'll come back to her later. The other shops were a butcher and a hairdresser. The post office was about two miles away. The main shopping area was in Cleveland a few miles away.

The house in Victoria Point

The house we stayed in was owned by a very large lady and her diminutive, balding husband (who didn't really say very much). She would say things like, 'Yes, dear,' or 'Can I help you my dear?'. I got a bit spooked by it. When I went into the shop she would say those things and I felt I couldn't get out of there fast enough. We had to go in to the shop as it was the only food shop for miles around. One day the husband seemed to have disappeared. The woman carried on as normal saying 'Can I help you dearie?', but the husband who had previously always been in the shop was nowhere to be seen. He had just simply disappeared. We never did see him again. Maybe he went on a long holiday. Who knows?

The mosquitoes got to me in Australia. Horrible little buzzy things which stung you all over and sucked your blood. You would always get bitten no matter what you did or how much you covered up. They seemed to pick on me and I scratched and scratched. This was the worst thing you could do, but try telling this to an eight year old who had never seen a mozzie before. I was covered in sores and they itched and itched and I cried and cried. I tried everything I could not to get bitten, but the blighters still bit me. I wore tight fitting pants and long sleeve shirts but it was no protections against those horrible little insects. I guess they stung me because I had rich blood coursing through my veins. The hot climate had not yet thinned my blood. It was going to be a year or two before I would be immune to mosquitoes.

We got used to living in Victoria Point after a while and I found it quite exciting. We hadn't made any friends as yet but it was early days. There was an island to explore and we visited it frequently. Mum made some friends when she was working on the farms and enjoyed socialising with

Relaxing on the beach at Coochiemudlo. Norma Bishop on left. Mum with no hat.

Mum (far right) Norma seated. As farm workers having a 'smoko' break.

them. A particularly good friend was Norma Bishop. She was also a Ten Pound Pom. They all worked on the farms doing various jobs, mainly picking gladioli flowers.

Everyone on the farm wore hats, except Mum. None of our family wore hats much in Australia. We never used sun cream so the hot weather burned our skin. The effects of the sun would be seen many years later. Both my parents had skin damage and they seemed to look ten years older than they were, very old and wrinkly before their time. We were not warned about the effects of the sun, even at school. I loved the sunshine and couldn't get enough of it.

Coochiemudlo was just one little island near where we lived. At the time I believe there were forty homes and ten families who lived there permanently. They were very nice houses. It seemed idyllic living on an island in the Pacific Ocean. The ferry operated on the weekends only, when we were there. We explored the island several times as the ferry ride wasn't too expensive and the trip only took about twenty minutes or so. We used to play in the mud flats near the enclosed beach and then go for a swim to wash it off.

There were enclosed areas in the sea where it was safe to swim. The enclosed area was made from interlocking wooden poles in the sea. This was safe from sharks but unfortunately not from jelly fish and we were stung quite a few times. The jelly fish were transparent and incredibly difficult to see until they stung you. I loved going to Coochiemudlo because we could muck about in the mud and go swimming and explore the island. Houses were cheap and I believe we could have bought one for a few hundred dollars. My father, not being an entrepreneur unfortunately didn't buy one, although we did have an opportunity to. One time, a local estate agents arranged a BBQ on the island for prospective customers. We all went and had a good BBQ, but Dad had no intention of buying as he didn't have any money. We only really went for the BBQ. I think there was only one shop on the island. Some of the other islands were Macleay Island and Stradbroke Island. We went to Stradbroke Island a couple of times. This was a much, much bigger island than Coochie, and many people lived there. We could only explore a small bit of it, and we needed to take the bus to look around. I thought it was really exciting to be able to explore these islands which were just right next to us. We had to go to nearby Cleveland to get a ferry to the island.

My brothers and I would take every opportunity to swim in the ocean, despite there being shark warnings. Victoria Point didn't have much in the way of sandy beaches, mostly mud flats. We would often dive off the jetty into the sea, or jump on the ferry and jump from there. The ferry man didn't like us doing this though and would shout at us to get off. I think we were pretty adventurous considering there were sharks swimming around.

The vast openness of Australia and where we lived appealed to me. It was something I had never experienced in England. We could roam around and explore things in complete freedom. I started fishing from the jetty which people went on to go by ferry to Coochiemudlo. There were usually a lot of fishermen on the jetty at the weekends, all with their

Our lovely Mum, sat on the rocks at Coochiemudlo

big rods, some fishing for shark. I thought this was really great as I had not fished before. In England we were so far away from the sea, I never really got to see it. So, at aged eight and a half I thought I would give fishing a go. No one taught me how to fish, I just sort of picked it up. All I had was a hand line with a bit of squid for bait. I dropped the line over the jetty and waited. I didn't wait too long before I got a bite. There was a really big tug on the line and I knew I had got something big. I was really excited. A few people left their fishing rods and crowded around me and were helping me to reel it in. I had caught a Yellow Tail. Or that's what they told me. I was super excited. I didn't have anything to put the fish in, and one of the guys told me to go and get a bucket. So I ran back to the house which was only a few hundred yards away. When I got back one of the older men had taken the hook out and I put the fish in the bucket. I noticed a load of guys were crowding round the spot where I had been fishing and were dropping their lines in exactly the same spot. I was happy to walk home with my catch, really proud of myself. We had the fish for tea that night and it fed the five of us. It got me hooked (excuse the pun) on sea fishing for years to come. Victoria Point was the best place to go fishing as it had a jetty. The long stretch between Victoria Point and O'Halloran Point was pretty much mud and stone, with the odd bit of sand.

Much later on I had a fishing trip with my older friend and a school friend. He had hired a boat and we all went from Victoria Point along the coast to Mooggurapum Creek. We only had hand lines although my older friend had a rod. My school mate swung his line round and round and unfortunately hit my older friend in his eye brow with the hook. Thankfully it wasn't serious and he managed to pull it out. It could have been serious though. After several hours of rowing, I only managed to catch one small fish, a small mackerel I think. Too small to eat so I had to throw it back. I never did catch another fish in Australia although I did try. What I did do after that was go crabbing. I don't know what got me into crabbing or why. I had never fished for crabs before, but I must have seen someone else doing it. I bought a crab net and I used to go to the local butchers for a bone. I figured to myself, 'Why should I spend hours fishing when I could just drop a crab net over the jetty and come back when the tide was going out a few hours later to find a great crab in the net?'. I put the bone in the net and chucked the net over the jetty and went home and did other things. Later, when I came back and pulled up the net, to my surprise I had caught a large sand crab. I took the net and crab back home with me and mum cooked it for tea. She never really liked doing it as she had to boil the crabs alive. She would leave the crab in the pot and walk away in another room as she couldn't bear to hear the scratching noises of the crab. However, when it was cooked the crab tasted delicious. I did quite a lot of crabbing at the Point. Sometimes I would catch mud crabs. They were just as big but had a different taste to them, not as tasty as sand crabs though. Mum and Dad used to call me 'Lobster pot'.

However, after a few weeks of crabbing, someone pinched my net and it was the end of my crabbing days. I couldn't afford another net. In any case we were not at Victoria Point for much longer and we would soon be moving to somewhere where I couldn't easily go fishing.

There was a public outdoor swimming pool not far away which I went to quite often. I first went there with Dad and the rest of the family. I thought I would dive in at the deep end and then swim to the shallow end. The only problem was, I didn't know how to swim. I dived in anyway. I couldn't feel the bottom (of course) and started to panic. I was drowning. I knew I was in trouble. Fortunately, Dad saw me, dived in and rescued me. There were no life guards in those days, so I was very fortunate. It put me off going in the deep end of the pool for a long time. I soon started to learn how to swim though.

A circus came to Victoria Point when we were there. There were real animals, trapeze artists and clowns. They allowed children to go on the horses as they were running around the ring. You were tied to a strap in case you fell off. I was able to ride a horse bareback and had a go and it was marvellous. I was strapped of course so if I fell off I would still just go whizzing around. It was probably a bit dangerous thinking about it. There was no health and safety in those days. It was great fun. I felt such freedom and exhilaration speeding around the tent. I loved the circus and still do.

At the show, there was a prize stall where you had to choose a number to win. I chose a number and to my surprise I won a toy car. It was a really big car, you could almost sit on it. I was super excited. Mum said she had a sense I would win something. Mum always seemed to have a sixth sense about things. Later on, she would tell me about things which she believed she saw.

Mum was very much interested in the news from England and used to keep up to date with what was happening. She said she knew all about the Profumo affair which was happening in 1963 in the UK when we were in Australia. She became very interested in the story and predicted Stephen Ward's death which unfortunately came true. She was very moved by the tragedy of it all and had a great empathy towards Stephen Ward whom she felt was betrayed by John Profumo and/or by the Establishment for political expediency. Also there was the assassination of President John F Kennedy. Being just eleven it didn't really affect me too much, but I knew it was very important and Mum and Dad were particularly affected by it. Over the years, I got to know more about it, and the conspiracy theories which followed.

Another move

The time had come for us to be on the move again. This was to be a predictable pattern for our family. I don't know why we were to move so many times. We would be leaving Victoria Point and moving to another place not too far away. I wasn't too disappointed. Our landlady was a bit too freaky for me and I had thoughts that she had done her husband in. There was something about her which didn't seem quite right.

Chapter Eight

O'HALLORAN POINT

So we were off to O'Halloran Point. It was just a few miles away, but nevertheless remote. We didn't have a car at the time, so we all had to carry our stuff along the beach and mud flats to our new house about two miles away. This was the shortest distance but there was no road or foot path along the coast and some of the mud flats we sank into were knee deep, while we were still trying to carry our stuff! Eventually we got to the house. It was a typical Australian wooden house built on stilts.

Houses in Australia were often elevated off the ground and erected on stilts or stumps, which was intended to withstand the harsh effects of flooding, heat, and insect infestations. Cooler air is drawn up from beneath the house by the elevated architecture, which helps to chill the residence. This was a much larger house than we had been in. We had very little furniture except for the bunk beds we had in East Brisbane. My parents had those, and we three children slept on a mattress on the floor. We had mosquito nets over the beds which stopped any mozzie getting in. Well it was supposed to, except it didn't. Somehow, when I would be just going off to sleep I would hear the familiar horrible buzzing noise. I could swear they were just waiting for me to be nearly asleep. I was too tired to bother swatting it. I knew it would bite me at some point during the night and I was right. Mosquitoes were the bane of my life in Australia. We were also plagued by cockroaches. They seemed to find a way into the house somehow. Horrible things. I would bash them with my shoe to kill them, but they would just crawl away. It didn't seem to matter how hard I hit them, they would just carry on crawling.

L to R: Giles, Walter and me with Mum and Dad. At our house in O'Halloran Point.

I was really excited about the new place as there was so much to explore. The house was in 36 acres of scrub land on the coast, built on a hill overlooking the ocean. There were all sorts of fascinating trees which I had never seen before such as Pawpaw and Bread Fruit trees. Pawpaw fruit tastes a bit like a banana with a hint of vanilla and mango. Delicious!

My brothers and I would go off and explore the place and roam around barefoot. I rarely wore shoes in Australia. Not many kids did wear shoes as it was too hot. It was at O'Halloran Point when I saw snakes for the first time. All sorts of snakes: large, small and multicoloured. I was terrified of them. Once, coming back from school, a long multicoloured snake was lying across the path and I was frozen to the spot. I didn't know what type it was or whether it was harmless or venomous. I wasn't prepared to find out. I waited for half an hour till it slithered away and I ran up the long path home. We had to be careful walking about barefoot through the long straw like grass. Once, I saw a huge snake from our house. It was lying on the grass several metres away and it was several inches thick and about six foot long. A huge thing. I stayed in the house, I was terrified. I looked again after an hour or so and it had disappeared. I don't know what type of snake it was. Often when walking through the bush, Dad carried a stick in case he saw a snake in the path. If he did he would beat it and kill it. Fortunately, we were never bitten, but I always kept a wary eye out for them.

There were other creatures as well. Some I had never seen or heard of in England. Once, a dingo scratched and howled at our door all night. We had kittens and it was trying to get them. It was very frightening especially when it let out it's piercing howl. In the morning, when we opened the door there were large claw marks where it had been scratching. Imagine the carnage if it had managed to get it. No one had warned us about dingoes at this time.

There was a wide verandah encircling the house. This was typical of houses in the region those days. Dad would often sit on an armchair on the verandah, looking out over the ocean and would sketch the scenery, usually in pastel. He loved to draw; he wasn't very good at it but he did try.

The path to the house from the main road was treacherous especially for vehicles. It was a long winding dirt track going uphill. There were lots of pot holes and boulders and it really was not suited for any form of traffic whatsoever. But we didn't have a car so it didn't really matter. However if any vehicle did try to venture to our house they would have a problem.

Dad and Mum found jobs working on farms. It was nearly all the work there was in this rural farming community. There were lots of different farms, mostly strawberry, but also for beans, cabbages and other crops and gladioli flowers. They would often work at different farms sometimes together but sometimes apart. Mum sometimes would pick gladioli on a Dutch owned gladioli farm. They didn't get much for a day's hard work, about £5. Of course it all depended on how hard you worked. Sometimes on a Saturday I would work for a day but I would only get about £2 no matter how hard I worked. Anyway it was enough for me, you could buy a lot for £2 back then.

It was hard, back breaking work and I really didn't know how my parents endured it for so many years. I don't think they had been used to such hard manual work. But they stuck it out. They made enough money to keep our heads above water so to speak but that was about all. The soil was very rich and fertile and perfect for growing. The area was called Redlands because of the rich red soil.

Otherwise, people had to drive to the city for work which was 22 miles away. There was only a small amount of other work than farming, such as teaching, shop work and fishing. I think my parents had a hard life, the work was tough and the pay low.

We were getting used to our way of life in Australia. We didn't have a TV at the time so we passed the time playing board games or card games. Dad would often tell me stories. They were very dark stories, usually by Edgar Alan Poe and they used to frighten me.

If we boys did anything wrong Dad would have this little game with us whereby he would send us 'to Coventry'. Which meant we were not to be spoken to by anyone for an indeterminate length of time. It could be hours or days. It was a pretty mean trick really as it really isolated us. I think he found it amusing. Mum would try to intervene in such situations when we saw Dad's worst side, but it didn't always work.

We learnt some of the songs and traditions of Australian life. *Waltzing Matilda* was a song we learnt and loved, although I was never too sure what a 'jolly jumbuck' was. There was no Google in those days to find out. I have recently learned a jumbuck is another name for a sheep.

Another favourite song was *Click Go The Shears*.

> Click go the shears boys, click, click, click,
> Wide is his blow and his hands move quick,
> The ringer looks around and is beaten by a blow,
> And curses the old snagger with the blue-bellied "Joe."

Again the words at the time were unfamiliar but, a ringer was stockman usually on a sheep or cattle farm, a snagger was an inexperienced shearer and a blue-bellied Joe: a ewe with little wool to shear!

Dad at O'Halloran Point. Skinny as a rake, he nearly always went shirtless

We felt we were becoming true Aussies. Except we weren't. I guess you can take the English person out of England but you can't take England out of the English person. We always felt English and were proud of it. But we knew we had to adapt and adapt quickly. As long as we didn't harp on about England to our mates we were ok. They didn't like it if we talked about England.

Australia was culturally laid back, relaxed and easy going; nevertheless the Australians worked hard and a person or a family could really make a go of it and become successful. I'm sure a lot of immigrants were very successful and made a good life for themselves. Get a good job, a nice car and a good salary. It didn't really work for my parents.

At O'Halloran Point there was no running water to rely on, there was only rain water. The rain water was collected in large cylindrical corrugated iron containers which could hold hundreds of gallons. Most houses had these. If there was no rain, there was no water. We had a well in the garden. The water wasn't suitable for drinking though. We would lower a bucket by rope and collect a bucket of water every so often and use the water for washing up. We didn't have a proper bath or shower. My dad lugged home a tin canoe he found at the beach and we used it for a bath. It leaked so you could only use it for a few minutes. Dad also made a tin bucket shower. He punched holes in the bucket, tied a rope to the handle and winched it up over a beam. We were only under there for just a few seconds before the bucket was empty. There was no hot water of course. Mostly if we wanted a wash we would wash in the sea. We had an outside toilet called the 'dunny'. I was always frightened to go especially at night because there would often be a snake in there. Dad would come down with me and check it was alright. It was a bit scary to go to at night and so if we wanted a pee we didn't bother with the dunny, we would go near the house.

At the beach with Dad, me on the left Giles and Walter

We didn't have anything or anyone to compare our lifestyles to. Some of my friends seemed to have a lot and lived in nice houses, but others seemed to have less than we did. Nearly everyone relied on rainwater. Only a few people owned a black and white TV. Not everyone had cars, hot running water, inside toilet or a house telephone. Well, at least none of the people I knew. There were some wealthy people but we were not usually invited to their homes. Mostly, it seemed, people were poor like us.

Dad was no good at DIY and couldn't really fix anything. There were lots of things which needed fixing, but he wasn't able to do it. There were several chicken runs and they were dilapidated. They could have been fixed and we could have had several chickens but Dad didn't have the skills to do it.

We often saw sharks. There was a small creek near where we lived at O' Halloran Point where we often went swimming called Eprapah Creek. Mum never went in but she just sat on the side watching to see if we were alright. Once, as I was coming out, she said she saw a shark's fin just gliding by. We also saw sharks in the ocean, particularly when we went on the ferry across to Coochiemudlo. It didn't deter me from going swimming though.

My parents rented the house for £2 a week. In hindsight, I wished we could have bought it back then, but it was not to be. My parents were not entrepreneurs nor did they have any business sense about them at all. Little did we realise in years to come where we lived would be prime development land and an area of outstanding natural beauty.

When I was nine or ten, I didn't really go out with my brothers, or Mum and Dad for that matter. On days off sometimes I would go to Brisbane. Not on my own, but there was an older guy who I went with. I can't remember his name, but he would be about 25. Mum thought it was a bit weird an older guy would want to go out with a child. I think she had words with him, which seemed to put her mind at rest. Looking back it seems a bit strange but I think he genuinely liked me. He would often pay for the bus ride into Brisbane, get me lunch and we would go to a film together. He seemed to like me for some reason. I did have a few other friends about my age, but found it difficult to relate to them. I was painfully shy with an inferiority complex. Probably because I desperately wanted to fit in to this strange culture I found myself in and partly because of discrimination. We were the Pommies. Not everyone called us Pommies but a few did. I think we were also discriminated against because we were poor. We couldn't afford even the most basic of things, like new clothes to wear. I hardly ever wore shoes in Australia, but then most of my friends didn't.

To further my education (especially as I found the education in school so poor) Aunt Kate sent me parcels containing 'Jackdaws' (named such as the bird liked to collect things). Jackdaws were a collection of information on historical events around the world, such as The Crimean War, The Battle of Waterloo, the Gunpowder Plot and so on. There was a lot of information with each of them, including copies of original letters, documents, historical facts, and many photographs. It was all very interesting, however, I was rather inundated with all of this over three or four years, and I had to write to Aunt Kate to ask her to stop sending me them as I couldn't take it all in. I thanked her for sending me them though. We were always taught to write a thank you letter to all of our relatives who had sent us presents and it's a thing I do to this day. Aunt Kate was very special and used to write to me in Australia. I used to treasure her letters. I would write to all my relatives and loved getting letters back from them. It was our only communication with the rest of the world.

Also, to help me improve my education my father bought me a subscription for books. They were children's classics and the authors ranged from Dickens to Shakespeare, Louisa May Alcott, and so on. I think I have about fifty of these books, all beautifully illustrated. They were printed by Reader's Digest. I am trying to reread them now as they are so good. I don't know why Dad bought them, just for me (and not for my brothers). Whether he thought I was the brainy one in the family or that I was special, I don't know. I don't think I ever thanked him for this, much to my regret. I am keeping them and passing them on to my children who I hope will value them as I have. I didn't know where the books had come from initially I thought they had come from someone else. But in hindsight it must have been a sacrifice for my parents as they had very little money. I did like books, probably not as much as my father, who was always reading something. However I did enjoy reading and studying. It is a legacy Dad passed on to me - the joy of reading plus an understanding that there are more important things than possessions - a love and appreciation of literature, poetry and the Arts.

Brisbane

I went with Dad to Brisbane a few times. Brisbane to me seemed such a big city in those days. I was fascinated by all the shops and stores and buildings. Dad enjoyed going to the city and went whenever he had the chance. I loved the city life (and still do). We went swimming in the Olympic pool in Brisbane. It was a massive pool, actually there were two or three of them. One was very deep, used for diving. I dived off the small board, but there was a series of diving boards which were Olympic standard. I went up a few steps, nearly to the top. I was too scared to go any further and I went down. When I got down I saw a little kid, younger than me, climb up to the very top and dive off the top platform without any fear. 'Geronimo!' he shouted. Dad swam the width of the pool right in the path of the high diving platform. Luckily no one was diving at the time, but a lifeguard shouted at Dad to get out of the way. I was embarrassed.

I had other reasons for going to Brisbane. I would regularly go to the dentist to have a look at my teeth and unfortunately get some fillings done. Although only eight years old, my parents never told us about oral hygiene as far as I knew, so I rarely cleaned my teeth. I'm not even sure I possessed a toothbrush. Both Mum and Dad never looked after their teeth. Mum had false teeth. She said she couldn't wait to have them all out. It was a bit strange. Dad only had a few, just two or three at the front. For some reason they didn't see teeth cleaning as a priority. I also ate sugar sandwiches and plenty of sweets. I didn't work out sugar could rot my teeth so didn't understand why I had to have so many fillings. Even the dentist didn't tell me to regularly brush my teeth. So I have a mouth full of fillings to this day. Now I brush my teeth regularly and they are all my own, thankfully.

My older friend and I watched a few movies in Brisbane. I remember watching *The Fall of the Roman Empire*. It was a really long film, and as I was leaving the cinema I felt totally disoriented. I enjoyed going to see films at the cinema. They were in full technicolour and we were unused to seeing it as we didn't own a TV at the time. It was like stepping into another world. I also watched *Ben Hur*, which had just been released at the time. I thought it was amazing. It's one of my favourite films to this day. I think it inspired me to become a Christian later on. It was powerful. Again, I came out of the film in a daze.

My brothers rarely came with me to Brisbane. I don't know why, I think they just got on with other things. Dad went to Brisbane a lot. He enjoyed the city life, and he found it a break from working on the farms.

Chapter Nine

VICTORIA POINT STATE SCHOOL

When we first arrived at Victoria Point we were quickly enrolled in the local school called Victoria Point State School. All of us three brothers were separated into different classes because of our ages. I was put into Grade 2, Giles was in Grade 1 and Walter in Grade 3. The grading system went up to Grade 7 at Primary school and from there you went to secondary school, usually aged about thirteen or fourteen. There were 30 or more boys and girls in the same class. One of my teachers at the school was a Mr Brown. He was a young man, and very Australian, but I did not find him to be a nice teacher. If coming to Australia was a culture shock, the school itself was another world for me.

He would laugh at me if I got anything wrong. I didn't mind so much if I had got something wrong, but if I hadn't been taught it, then I objected. We were asked to construct a sentence with the word 'passer-by'' in it. I really didn't know what the word meant. No one had told me. My sentence was 'He passerby the hospital.' Mr Brown saw it and read it out to the whole class and laughed his head off, as did others. But he never told me what it meant. He just said, 'Oh, that sounds really Australian, doesn't it?' I didn't really get the joke. I just wanted to smack him one. Was I being overly sensitive? Probably. But it's still not nice to be embarrassed in front of everyone in the class. Maybe it was a great toughening up exercise. It should have helped me grow up, but it didn't. I just felt shame and insecure.

A copy of our school register at Victoria Point State School.

Mr Brown was someone who should have never been in teaching or any job which involved people, especially children. He seemed to have a particular dislike for me and one or two others in the class. He took great delight in caning boys for no apparent reason. He would bring us out to the front of the class, to embarrass us in front of everybody and then get his cane and whack us over the hand a few times. One lad was hit so hard his hand started bleeding. Mr Brown didn't seem too bothered by this and seemed to rather enjoy it. Some of the girls liked him and thought he was really good looking. But then they were never beaten. This school was a horrible wake-up call. It was like 'Dotheboys Hall' in Dickens' *Oliver Twist*. It seemed to belong to the last century. I was too busy trying to avoid being caned to actually learn anything. I was in a constant state of fear and shame. Fear, because the teachers liked to punish me or insult me for no reason. Shame, because we were poor and we were so called English Poms. How could I learn anything anyway? Corporal punishment seemed to be the norm in Australian Schools at the time. I think it was a cruel punishment because it was usually done in front of the whole class so everyone would see me getting the cane and knew why I was getting punished. The punishment was usually unjust which made it worse and brought me more shame and embarrassment not to mention anger at the injustice of it all. I hated my teachers. Most of them anyway. A friend of mine, Peter, who sat next to me in class was told off for not writing in his book what the teacher thought he should have written. The teacher didn't know he had written it down in the class like another teacher told him to. The teacher thought he hadn't. He would accept no explanation from my friend but told the lad to stand up on the chair and proceeded to whack his legs with a ruler. My friend started to cry. I should have stuck up for him, but I was too scared to. I knew if I said anything I would get whacked too. I was so fed up with being whacked all the time, I kept quiet. These things stay with you for life.

Of course, I have forgiven my teachers but I don't forget. I can say in every instance of me getting the cane or the leather strap it was always unwarranted and unjust. This is the real shame of it and it was always a public shaming. At aged nine, I was accused of cheating (I didn't) and I got the cane for it. It made a negative impression at a time when I was still very young and impressionable.

Some of the teachers must have thought I was really dim. They didn't seem to encourage me or say anything positive. I would react according to their expectations. They didn't exactly inspire me to do great things. There seemed to be a lot of prejudice. I couldn't say it was true everywhere in the country, I just think as we were in a very rural area which seemed to attract teachers who were just not good at their job. At East Brisbane State School the teaching was very different and there was no prejudice against us being English. The teachers there were very good and very supportive, which all helps a child to learn. Strangely enough, the girls were never caned or disciplined in any way. I expect they were too nice. Or maybe there was an unwritten rule: teachers do not cane girls. Also, as far as I know none of the female teachers used the cane on anyone. The female teachers were often very good, but they were all so young and inexperienced: probably in their early twenties.

One time a boy's mother came in to one of the classes as the teacher was in the middle of teaching. She grabbed him by the collar and in front of all the children and said, 'If you every touch my boy again, I'll kill you'. The teacher was understandably shocked. I'm not sure what happened to his lesson afterwards.

Victoria Point State School Register of Corporal Punishment

Another teacher, Mr Smith, took a particular dislike to the three of us brothers for some reason. We never really got on the right side of him (if there was a right side). Whether he knew what was going on in the classrooms I do not know. He would also administer swift justice with his leather strap and quite frequently too. Unbeknown to me, he had 'spies', boys he recruited, to spy on kids in the playground to see if they said or did anything wrong. One of these spies thought I said something to a Dutch lad and I was hauled off to the headmaster where I got whacked. No explanation or pleading innocence would suffice. 'Justice' was swift. It was all very confusing for an eight year old, who had left his home country and friends and relatives landing in a strange place where everybody in authority seemed out to get you. The irony was I was accused of discrimination. And all the time the school, from headmaster to teachers and some of the kids, were discriminating against us.

'Pommie B * * * * * *' some of them would say. I guess most of my learning was trying to figure out how to survive this new place. There was more to come.

It was no use trying to pretend to be Aussies, not with our English accents. But why would I want to anyway? I was proud of being English. I didn't want to hide my identity. Why should I? I had nothing to be ashamed of. A young lad came up to me at school once and I was talking about Winston Churchill and how he helped to win the Second World War. He didn't like this and scoffed at the mention of Churchill's name saying something derisory. I learnt it was best to keep my mouth shut, instead of saying anything about England. But I wondered who fed him negative information about the war, Churchill and England in general. Was it his parents or his teachers maybe?

In my second year of school, I wrote a play. It was about cowboys. I had typed it up on Mum's old typewriter. The teacher, to my surprise, let me act out the play with some other kids in the class. It went pretty well I believe. Finally, I thought, I was gaining some credibility. Another teacher came in to have a look so it couldn't have been bad at all. I wrote another play later on, *Snow White and the Seven Dwarfs,* for which I received a prize. The prize was an introduction to a pen pal from Japan. I didn't even know where Japan was. But I was given some money for a stamp to Japan and I wrote him a letter. I still remember it after all these years. I wrote to him (or her) - I never did get to find out, and had just one reply. I gave up after that.

We had to do handwriting practice at school. I enjoyed this very much. We were given books which had copperplate writing in and we had to copy it exactly into our books. It was quite difficult but I really liked getting it absolutely right. We would spend hours writing away. We had an ink pot on the desks and we would dip our pens in the ink and write. An inspector came round one time when I was busy copying. He told me how to use the pen for better accuracy. This one bit of interest really inspired and helped me. Now, I love fine writing or calligraphy as it's called. I'm glad children are still taught handwriting, though I have seen children hold a pen in many strange ways.

During our lunch breaks we would play in the school playground, which was a large open field. Part of it was a football field, and another an area for rounders and a shady area of trees. Often I would play marbles with the other kids. We seemed to devise all sorts of games with marbles. One game was called 'Poison'. If you hit someone's marble with yours they were out. The next person could then swap their marble for something much smaller even a seed. I managed to knock everyone out. Then finally there was one person left. He swapped his marble for a seed and from about four feet away I flicked my marble up in the air and it landed fair and square on the seed. I won about 30 marbles that day. I was very pleased with myself, and for once I got a bit of kudos. We would take sandwiches to school and I nearly always had peanut butter and Vegemite®. There was a snack van which came round to the school at lunchtimes. I didn't buy much from the person, but once I bought a meat pie. It was lukewarm and when I ate it I was physically sick. I didn't buy anything from the van again.

School was fairly boring but I did settle in eventually. We learned Maths by rote, especially all the times tables. When we marched (yes, marched) from one class to another we recited the times tables - two twos are four, two threes are six and so on. I got pretty good at it and quite enjoyed maths. We also learned sentence structure and grammar. I was able to identify all the various components of any sentence. I remember there were a lot of lessons about the topic and we were forever trying to analyse sentences. Subject, predicate, nouns and verbs. Also the different clauses and so on. Information I have nearly forgotten about now. Probably just as well.

The teachers talked a lot about Australia. We never did learn about English History. It was all about who explored Australia. Who crossed Australia from South to North (Burke and Wills), who incidentally both died on the return journey (which seemed to me to be a bit of a pointless exercise). Who crossed it from East to West? (Edward John Eyre). Facts I remember to this day. Who discovered the gold mines at Kalgoorlie and Coolgardie, when they were discovered and by whom. I often wished I had discovered them myself. Often, our classes would be doubled up so there would be about sixty children in a class with one teacher. This is probably another reason why we didn't learn much.

Every morning all the pupils would be lined up outside the school as if on parade. The teachers would be there as well. It was like a military exercise. There the headmaster would lecture us on something or other. Once, he told all the boys off for looking up at the girls as they were walking up the stairs. Of course, what did the boys do straight after? After the five minute lecture we would then have to sing the national anthem and all of us had to march to our respective classes in military fashion under the strains of *Advance Australia Fair* or some other Australian song played on an old tinny record player. I don't remember them playing 'God Save Our Gracious Queen'.

> 'Australian sons let us rejoice
> For we are young and free',
> Australians all let us rejoice,
> For we are one and free;
> We've golden soil and wealth for toil,
> Our home is girt by sea;

> Our land abounds in Nature's gifts
> Of beauty rich and rare;
> In history's page, let every stage
> Advance Australia fair!
> In joyful strains then let us sing,
> Advance Australia fair!

We had to sing these songs as they were being played. I didn't know whether I could really sing it as technically I wasn't an Australian son!

So I felt a certain stigma. I couldn't verbalise how I was feeling as a young child, but you just grow up feeling that certain people don't like you. I found this difficult because I wanted people to like me, but I didn't know how I could achieve this. I was rubbish at sports. I think because I never did any sports before coming to Australia. Then I was thrust into this outdoor, sporting culture the Australians love so much. Yet, to me it was all foreign. Playing cricket or rugby, rounders, tennis or football were all new to me. I was expected to know how to play. Often, I would be standing in a line of kids waiting to be picked for their team by one of two oversized sporting heroes called Captains. Standing next to me would be a vastly overweight kid or another one so skinny he could be blown over by a small gust of wind. Almost without fail these captains would pick these kids and I would be the last to be picked. 'Oh come on then Oldershaw, if we must have you,' they would say. It made me feel really important! Consequently, I never really got into sports. I thought 'blow you mate, I'm not going to be embarrassed by you again.' I didn't enjoy team sports for this reason. Many years later, I would take up running, which I enjoy to this day. To further put me off team sports, a teacher, who should have known better, bawled me out one time in front of everyone because I didn't know where to stand in a tennis court.

There were four of us on the tennis courts and we were supposedly playing doubles. I apparently stood in the wrong place, which was a real crime.

'He doesn't know where to stand', he bawled to everyone.

'Great, because you never told me where to stand,' I thought. I felt stupid but also angry.

Once in the playground, I was just minding my own business, walking around, and a group of girls were playing rounders. Suddenly, I got hit in the jaw by a rounders ball. The girl had hit the ball and managed to swing the bat around behind her so the ball hit me full force in the jaw. Blood was everywhere. I was nearly knocked out and blood all over my face. The girl never said sorry, just 'Why didn't you look where you were going?' Before I knew it one or two kids took me to a sink and sponged the blood off. I think they must have put a plaster on it. The cut was never stitched which it should have been and I have a scar to this day.

We also played cricket. I didn't mind this so much and I think I was reasonably okay. It was the first time I had played cricket and I had to quickly learn the rules. I was pretty good at bowling and at least the teachers didn't tell me off for doing something I shouldn't have done. One of the lads got a left hook with a ball fair and square on the jaw, just like me. He survived too. Another lad was bowled out and as soon as the ball hit the wicket a kookaburra laughed in the trees somewhere.

This was how school was in those days. I'm pleased to say Victoria Point State School is not like this today. The reviews are very positive and the teaching staff are excellent. But back in the sixties it was not a great learning environment.

Walking to school

It was about a two mile walk to school from O'Halloran Point, but it seemed a lot longer. We either went by road which was the long way round, or we cut across farmers' fields. The farmers didn't like it though and would tell us off if they saw us. However, if we went by road we would come up against some Alsatian dogs kept by an old Aboriginal living in a tin shack. The dogs would often chase us and try to bite us. I had a bike which I sometimes used to go to school and back, but the dogs would definitely chase after me then and nip me on my heels. This was a bit of a problem because we always went barefoot. Once Mum cycled back this way from work and was bitten on her leg by one of the dogs. The bite was so severe, Mum fell off her bike. A farm worker nearby looked over and said 'Are you alright missus?'

She was far from alright. The bite was deep with blood everywhere. Mum eventually got to a hospital. I'm not sure how she got there, she must have used someone's house phone to ring for an ambulance. There were no mobiles back then. She came back home later on that evening, after being given a penicillin injection at the hospital. However, unbeknown to her, she was allergic to penicillin and gradually during the evening at home her face and throat started to swell. It was so bad she found it difficult to breathe and it was getting worse. Dad rushed out to the nearby neighbours to use their telephone and call an ambulance. When Dad came back he asked each of us three children to go in and kiss Mum goodbye. He thought it was the end. We could sense the fear in Dad. Dad then had to go to the start of the dirt track leading up to the house to direct the ambulance driver. We children were left alone with Mum who was dying. There were no outside lights, it was pitch black, no road markings or anything and just a single track road in the middle of the bush.

I was really scared and didn't know what to do. My brothers didn't know what to do. I had not seen Mum like this and I didn't know what dying meant. Fortunately, the ambulance eventually arrived, late in the night and the paramedics were able to take Mum to hospital to treat her and she survived. It was a very scary time for us. My Dad was worried all night and so were we. The Alsatian dogs were put down. I didn't know it then but if the ambulance hadn't come when it did, just half an hour later Mum would have died.

Christmas

We had our first Christmas at O'Halloran Point. It was very different from what we were used to in Egland: the freezing cold and snow. Here, it was the middle of summer. They still had Santa Claus at Christmas. Poor old Santa would be seen sweating away in the tropical heat with all his robes and false beard on standing on a street corner wishing everyone a 'Merry Christmas'. We boys still believed in Father Christmas despite the fact no houses had chimneys for him to climb down.

One Christmas, Walter had put out a little drink and a mince pie for Santa. When Walter woke up in the morning, he realised Santa hadn't drunk the sherry or eaten the mince pie he had put out for him. Walter was very disappointed and upset that Santa had ignored his generous offering. Somehow, Christmas didn't seem like Christmas. It didn't seem right that we could go out in the hot sunshine and swim in the sea.

We usually got presents from our Aunts and Uncles. We each of us got a small present and some board games. Mum and Dad would get money sent across which meant we could have a decent Christmas dinner.

On the jetty at Victoria Point. Giles on left, then Walter and me..

We would put a stocking out and would find a packet of crisps, an apple, an orange, a dinky toy of some sort and a small bar of chocolate. We thought it was great. We were so excited as we opened our stockings. We would also get a main present and the first Christmas we got some toy guns sent over from England. I got a great big revolver, Walter got a rifle and Giles got a gun. Walter also got a real rifle which fired pellets. We used the rifle a lot, shooting at various things: tin cans, trees and so on. We loved the games we got for Christmas. We didn't have a TV then and so had to amuse ourselves with the games or go play outside.

A few days after Christmas, we realized our house had been burgled. We had come back from school and found things scattered all over the place. All our Christmas presents were stolen. The special toy guns we got, and other presents had gone. I think it must have been kids because there were some valuable books and paintings on the wall (one by Stanley Spencer) and other items which were left untouched. It was a shame because those Christmas presents were all we had. We didn't have any house security. There were no locks on the doors, so anybody could have walked in while we were out. However, despite this incident, we enjoyed the Christmases we had in Australia although so very different to England.

Setting fire

One event which took place while we were at O'Halloran Point, I will never forget. My Dad and I were walking up from the beach. Our house was on a hill and we walked up the dirt path towards the house. We had been swimming in the sea and trying to cool down on a very hot day. Half way up the dirt track my Dad stopped. I didn't know what he was stopping for initially. It was the height of summer and the long grass was tinder dry. All 36 acres of it. Dozens of trees and bushes. He suddenly got out a box of matches.

Dad was a smoker and used to smoke about twenty cigarettes a day. I had a sense he was going to do something because he had this look in his eyes. I couldn't do anything to stop him, I was only nine years old. He suddenly lit a match. I said, 'No, Dad don't do it!' But it was too late. 'It's alright' he said. He threw the match on the dry straw. I couldn't stamp it out quick enough. In any case if I did he would have been mad at me. The fire took hold and quickly spread. I took to my heels, racing home to warn my Mum and brothers. By the time I got home it was too late to do anything but watch this awful conflagration. It was late in the afternoon and the fire burned for hours. It burnt all through the night and nearly reached our house. We all had to stay up for most of the night outside. Mum was fuming. I didn't have to tell Mum what Dad had done, she already knew. We all got buckets of water to wet the ground around us and make sure the flames didn't come near the house. I don't think our efforts would have done much good though if the fire had got to the house. We heard later the fire could be seen for miles around. There were no fire engines nearby and we had to do the best we could to put it out. But all we could do was to let the fire burn. In the morning the whole area was black and scorched, everything burnt. It was the talk of the school the next day. I was very sorry the fire had burnt all the scrub land we used to play in, and scorched all the trees, killing some of the small ones and also some of the wildlife. I realised then my father was obsessed by fire. I didn't have much respect for my father after this.

So that traumatic event came and went. Over the weeks the grass and bushes grew back, but it was never quite the same.

Me walking up from the beach at O'Halloran Point.

Chapter Ten

CORPORAL PUNISHMENT IN AUSTRALIA

I thought I would just mention about corporal punishment in Australia and the current situation. Interestingly, Queensland (the state I grew up in) is the only state in Australia which still allows corporal punishment in non-state schools.

It seemed, in Australian schools corporal punishment was the standard form of correction. Did it do me any lasting harm? Although I didn't like it at the time, I don't think it really affected me later on in life. The only harm I felt was at the time it seemed I was generally caned for no good reason. The teachers seemed to spot something in me which I didn't believe was there. It was done so publicly which was highly embarrassing. Nobody likes to have to stand on a chair in front of everyone and be accused of something you may (or may not have done) and then get publicly caned for it; all eyes staring at you. Not only do you resent being caned, but you soon resent the teacher who is doing the caning. All of which doesn't put you in a good frame of mind for learning.

It has only been relatively recently, in the mid 1990s, that corporal punishment has been banned as a practice in most Australian schools.

There has been extensive research into the effects of corporal punishment on children. There is strong evidence to suggest physical punishment harms children's cognitive, behavioural, social and emotional development, particularly later on in life. Evidence also suggests physical punishment does not reduce defiant or aggressive behaviour nor does it promote long term positive behaviour in children. In fact, a systematic review on the use of physical punishment in schools found it had negative effects on the academic performance of children resulting in behavioural issues, such as antisocial, aggressive and violent behaviour. Other negative effects include mental health and emotional problems, including low self-esteem. Stress can be a big factor in affecting brain development and the threat of corporal punishment adds stress. My main concern was the abuse of it, which in my case I felt it was.

Following a review in 2011, the recommendation was made to introduce a full prohibition of corporal punishment within the family in all states and territories. The Government rejected the recommendation, stating: 'While Australia has programs in place to protect children against family violence, and laws against assault, it remains lawful for parents in all States and Territories to use reasonable corporal punishment to discipline their children.'

In Queensland, under the Criminal Code Act section 280, corporal punishment is lawful in schools under the provisions for reasonable force stating that 'It is lawful for a parent or a person in the place of a parent, or for a schoolteacher or master, to use, by way of correction, discipline, management or control, towards a child or pupil, under the person's care such force as is reasonable under the circumstances'.

All corporal punishment, however mild or light, carries an inbuilt risk of escalation. Studies suggest that parents who used corporal punishment are at heightened risk of perpetrating severe maltreatment.

Until the 1970s, the opinion of the Queensland educational system was that corporal punishment was a necessary evil to be used as a last resort.

Public opinion supported this view and objections were mainly targeted at violations of the regulations.

Author J Landon reported in his textbook, *School Management*, '*Pain was an inefficient form of punishment which frequently was wasteful of nervous energy, had a weakening effect, built up hatred and also hardened pupils to its use so that it became less effective.*' It is generally felt in educational circles skilled teachers do not need to use this type of punishment except on extraordinary occasions, but often less capable teachers were more dependent upon it. In my experience at school this definitely seemed to be true plus, I think the large class sizes had a bearing on the use of corporal punishment.

Landon's book also reported, '*Though some schools had given up using the cane, other forms of bodily pain had been substituted, for example kneeling on the floor, supporting weights for a long time and being goaded by sharp points. It was better for the head teacher alone to inflict corporal punishment. This would ensure that it was in the hands of an experienced teacher whose uniform standard of punishment would be more readily accepted by the pupils. A cane was the best instrument to use and it should be kept out of sight. No good teacher walked around with a cane in his hand.*'

From about 1914 to the late 1940s, The Suggestive Handbook of Practical School Method was the preferred book on behaviour management. The section on corporal punishment remained unchanged for over thirty years, stated '*that there were a few scholars for whom a little corporal punishment was the best and only effective corrective.*' Most forms of physical reprimand were considered to be harmful and unfair. If such punishment was inflicted without vindictiveness, it could have positive results and be beneficial to correction of misdeeds and get positive results from the offender and the class overall.

In the 1960s and 1970s, there was a explosion of text books on methods of teaching (primarily from American and Great Britain) which were used in Queensland tertiary institutions. In these, additional research evidence was presented in support of the abolition of corporal punishment, but many of the texts supported its use for serious offences when all other methods have failed.

From my own recent research into the practice, despite the laws allowing the non-state sector to use corporal punishment, there is no evidence to suggest the practice is happening in Queensland, it just means in theory a non-government school is at liberty to use it.

The Queensland Government said its Department of Education and Training does not have the authority to determine policy for the non-state education sector, but it said policies banning the practice in state schools have been in place since 1995.

Alan Corbett, former teacher and Australian politician, said policies are not enough, and the law as it stands leaves it open for corporal punishment to be reintroduced in religious or independent schools.

It was only in April 2016 the Christian Community Ministries Ltd (CCM) directed the thirteen schools it owns across Australia to stop using corporal punishment.

Chapter Eleven

MY SPIRITUAL SEARCH

Several instances in my childhood set me on a spiritual search. I wasn't aware I was seeking anything spiritual at the time but I've always been a deep thinker. I believed in God whoever He was and would sometimes pray to Him. One thing which bothered me as a boy was an incident in England. I had gone to a corner shop just near our house in Badgers Close. I think I went in with a friend. Anyway I pinched a bar of chocolate and walked out. No one saw me do it. It was worth sixpence at the time (six old pence). I managed to get away with it, but I felt so guilty I never ate it. Instead, I hid it in a bridge somewhere nearby. I never told my parents or anyone about it at the time, but I still felt guilty doing it. When we were in O'Halloran Point, we were having dinner around the table like we always did. We were talking about events in our lives. I mentioned about this incident to my family. I felt really guilty again, as if the situation wasn't really resolved. It brought everything back and I felt real shame and guilt. I rushed away from the table and went to bed, crying and fearful. My Dad tried to console me as best he could. He said 'It's alright, don't worry.' But I said to Dad, 'The devil's got me and saying I've got you now.' Dad didn't know what to say to me. He just kept saying, 'Don't worry, it's alright.' But it didn't seem to help much. I don't know where my sense of guilt had come from. I had never been to Church. My parents did not go to church or encourage us to in any way. I didn't know much about God or the Bible or anything religious. It was something my parents didn't talk about. They were moral people but the important things to them were to speak properly (whatever that meant), how to eat with our knives and forks, to sit properly at the meal tables, only talk when asked to do so and to have good manners, 'Manners maketh man'. God was rarely mentioned, so I really didn't know what to do with these feelings. This sense of guilt stayed with me for years.

We were never given religious education in school but I knew there was a God. I just didn't know I could have a relationship with Him. If anything, I thought being a Christian was some sort of intellectual response or some sort of sense of duty. I thought it involved trying to go to Church every Sunday and trying to be good.

Little did I know at the time, but I was on a spiritual search, troubled with feelings of guilt. My guilt feelings were never resolved until I became a Christian in New Zealand.

I started asking myself a lot of questions about life even at a young age. Who am I? Why am I here? What's life all about? No one seemed to give me any answers.

While we were living at Link Road in Victoria Point I went to church. I only went a couple of times though. It was an Anglican Church and it was rather stuffy and boring. The children were led out during the service to another room and we huddled round a table. The Sunday School teacher read a story out of a Reader's Digest booklet. I'm not sure what he read from the booklet, but it didn't seem to be anything to do with God or Jesus. I thought it was a bit weird and it didn't make any sense to me anyway. So I stopped going. My church attendance was very short lived. A few months later I heard about a boys' camp run by the Methodist Church. It was a week long camp so I went. My brothers didn't go, just me. It was somewhere close to Brisbane, I can't exactly remember where. We were in a dormitory with about four bunk beds in each room.

I remember twins stayed in the same room: their beds were immaculate. We all had to make our beds in the morning, and even the underneath of their beds was immaculate, all the blankets folded neatly. I don't know how they did it. It was a very boring week for me though. We didn't seem to do much. We went on a hike once and we had lots of meetings where we had to learn passages from the Bible. I still remember some of those verses. I was not allowed to go into the swimming pool because of some sores on my leg due to mosquito bites. This was annoying for me because it was incredibly hot and dry. I'm afraid it put me off church and religion for a long time. I thought it was all a bit boring really. I didn't go on the camp again and I stopped going to church.

Yet, lots of things would come crowding in to my mind, crowding out these other thoughts. Like still getting familiarised with the Australian way of life. Still trying to make friends, trying not to get caned at school and learn new subjects. It wasn't easy and we were constantly on the move. I still had my doubts, struggles and insecurities, so I forgot about God for a while. It seemed God didn't forget about me.

Earlier, I mentioned how the film Ben Hur left me in a daze. After coming out of the daze it made me question and want to know more. I wanted to know who this Jesus was. He was mentioned at school; he was in the film but I didn't know Him. This got me really thinking.

Chapter Twelve

LINK ROAD

Not long after the fire incident we were on the move again. I'm not sure why and I had started to enjoy O'Halloran Point. We moved to a smaller house on Link Road. It was much closer to Victoria Point and to school. It was to be our last Australian house move and we stayed until 1966. Even though it was a smaller house, with a small garden we still had lots of land to explore and it was only a few hundred yards to the beach at the back of the house. The house was made of prefabricated material and built on stilts. We had a sink which we used as a bath and an outside toilet. The 'Dunny' men used to come once a week to empty it. What a job, phew! However, we would not go there at night but the male members of the family would pee from the verandah. Needless to say the grass was scorched!

We got our first TV (which was black and white of course) in 1962. I would be aged about nine and a half and the year was 1962. I started making a few friends. I had a friend called John Barker who lived in a posh house, much posher than us. I used to go round there occasionally and play. Other friends I recall are David Swingler; he was a ginger-haired, friendly, nice guy. Steven Pakinotice, was our next door neighbour a few hundred yards down the road and I used to go around with him a lot. He was about the same age and in the same class as me. Steven Pakinotice (or as Mum used to say 'Steven Pack up your notice') was of Italian descent. We used to go swimming together or just hang out going for bike rides. I felt a bit sorry for him as his parents gave him a hard time. One time while I was at this house his mother bawled him out for some reason and she told him he would have to turn over a new leaf and change his ways. I thought he was already a fairly decent chap. She went on and on, and I thought it was unfair considering I was there. It was embarrassing too. They had a small holding and had several chickens. Once when I was there, Steven took a chicken and with an axe chopped it's head off. I was shocked. Even more shocked when the chicken kept on running around without its' head on.

Another 'friend' was a guy called Alan Smith. I think he was a troubled lad. He had no father and was brought up by his young mother. He had two younger sisters. He used to try and bully me, and most times when I went round to his place he would want to wrestle me for some reason. He was stronger than me and would often beat me. I couldn't see why he wanted to do it, but I felt I had to humour him. He wasn't really a nice guy, a bully really. Anyway, over time I drifted away from his friendship. His family though were nice and friendly.

We had our first bonfire night at Link Road. The fireworks on sale were different to the ones you can buy now. The bangers, as we called them, were huge, like sticks of dynamite. There was no health and safety warnings about the dangers of using fireworks. We would put these 'bangers' under an empty baked bean can and watch it explode lifting the can thirty feet into the air. It was great fun. It's a wonder we didn't get blown up ourselves. I nearly did. I had one of those bangers in my hand and I must have been distracted. I had lit the fuse but took a while to throw it away. It blew up in my hand. Fortunately it didn't do any damage just frightened me a lot and now I am very careful about fireworks and the dangers of them.

When I was ten or eleven I would go out on the farms on some Saturdays and spend the day picking strawberries or beans or whatever was needed. I would get paid £2 a day for it. It was hard work and I would be on my knees all day crawling around strawberry plants and inching my way to the next one. I really earned my pay! I then found other ways of making money; doing odd jobs for people. I would go round knocking on doors and asking a 'bob a job'. I didn't get a lot of money doing this and I got a lot of refusals but some people would take me on for a few shillings.

Taken at our house in Link Road. Giles on left, Walter (seated) me on right and Dad.

In those days it was pounds, shillings and pence in those days; decimal currency didn't come in till 14th February 1966. I know the time well from a jingle the government put out.

In come the dollars, in come the cents

To replace the pounds and the shillings and the pence

Be prepared folks when the coins begin to mix

On the 14th of February 1966

Opposite our house on the other side of the road stood a corrugated metal shack. In the shack, lived three generations of Aboriginals, called the Coolwells. We got to know them very well. For all Dad's foibles he was never prejudiced. We all made friends with this family and we used to enjoy hanging out with them. We would go bike riding together and swimming in the local creek. They were a bit older than me but we really got on together. Sometimes the kids came round to play, and adults

The Coolwell family. The girl on the left is Gwen and the girl on the right Elsie.

visited too. Dad welcomed them into our house, which wasn't the done thing in sixties Australia. One old fellow came in to the house and sat on the floor. He was worse the wear for drink and he was expounding on spirits and aboriginal beliefs and so on. I didn't really understand what he was talking about, but he was ok and no problem and eventually left. Unfortunately, the older Aboriginal men did like to drink and the cheapest way of drinking was to drink methylated spirits mixed in with a bit of milk. It must have tasted disgusting. The Aboriginals were heavily discriminated against. They wouldn't be allowed in certain shops or places of entertainment or the local swimming pool. I couldn't understand why. I used to go around with them, going on cycle rides together. There were a couple of girls I particularly liked who were very pretty; Elsie and Gwen. Once Elsie invited me into the shack where they lived. The first thing which hit me was the smell. It was the smell of stale sweat. It was also very dark and gloomy. I could just about see an old lady in her bed and a couple of other people. They were very polite. I was scared. I had to go, and I left in a bit of a hurry.

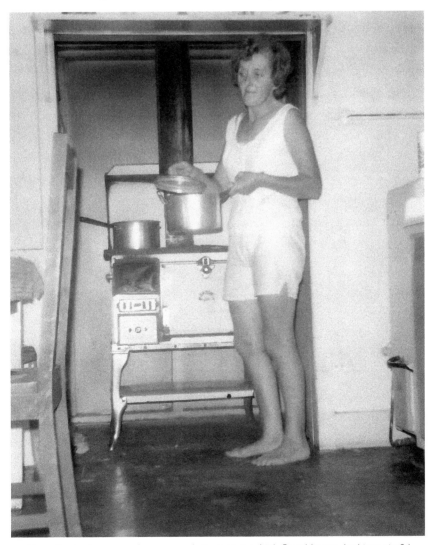

Mum, preparing a meal on a wood stove at our Link Road house, looking wistful.

About this time I liked to listen to Elvis Presley and his music. I was sitting in a shack with a couple of Aboriginal friends listening to his music and I thought it was great. I remember songs like *Jailhouse Rock* and *All Shook Up*.

My Dad wasn't so impressed by the popular music being played. He had grown up listening to classical music. He didn't enjoy pop music and wouldn't let us listen to it, but would play his classical music. He never did understand contemporary pop music, he thought it was all rubbish. 'Turn that rubbish off', he would say. Mum was the same and she would often say, "Turn it down". She was much more used to listening to Vera Lynn or other war time classics. The Beach Boys had released *Surfin USA* which I liked to listen to and of course The Beatles were on the scene. My Aunt Woozle, sent me a postcard of The Beatles and she wrote on it, 'These boys sound like a good band'. Little did she realise how big they were to become. They did a tour in Australia in 1964 while we lived there. I was twelve and I wasn't really into The Beatles at that stage, but as time progressed and I got into my teenage years, and listened to more of their music I thought they were great. Probably the best band ever and they came from England!

Mum, proudly showing off our utility vehicle..

My parent's disapproval of pop music didn't stop us listening to it, although we had to find other ways, like when Dad and Mum were out of the house. Then we would listen to our pop music on the radio and it was great. The sixties were a tremendous time for music. The pop music coming from England and America seemed a long way off from us in Australia but I loved listening to all the songs, from the different artists. My favourite was Elvis Presley. He had such a beautiful voice.

During the time we were living at Link Road, we went on a trip to the Gold Coast. It was our first (and only) family holiday in Australia and it was just for one day. It was about 22 miles away, south of Brisbane on the East coast. Dad had bought an old pick-up truck. We three kids had to sit in the back of the pick-up with Mum and Dad in the front. It wasn't a very good journey because the back of the pick-up was very uncomfortable and Dad drove very erratically.

When we got there, it was beautiful. Lovely, long, sandy beaches. We were at Surfer's Paradise. I don't think I fully appreciated it at the time, but this was the Mecca for all surfers from Australia and around the world. I looked around the shops and bought myself a name tag with my name on it. 'Bobby'. Despite the horrible journey, we had a really good day. Later, I gave the name tag and chain to Elsie when we left Australia to go to New Zealand. More about that later.

At our Link Road house there was a local creek which we used to swim in. It was called Moogurrapum Creek. It was said by the locals to be bottomless. I'm sure it was an old wives tale or rather local legend, but it must have been very deep. Several of us kids went down to swim in it. My two brothers, Walter and Giles, along with some of the Aboriginals and a few others. There was a hilly area where we could jump from about twelve feet high. We were not scared of swimming in this large creek, but realized there could be sharks and other nasty creatures swimming about. However it didn't seem to put us off. We went back several times and had a great time larking about.

Walter was always up to tricks, always experimenting with things. One day he said he wanted to douse me in petrol and set light to me. Fortunately I had the presence of mind (even at ten) to say 'No'. I didn't think it was a good idea. 'Oh, go on Bob', he said. 'it won't hurt you, there's a vapour between your skin and the flames which will protect you'. It all sounded very plausible and Walter was convinced. But I wasn't, thankfully, which is why I live to tell the tale. Later, he would find electrical lamps he had 'repaired'. He would ask Giles and I to test them out by putting our finger on the socket. We got an electric shocks every time and Walter was pleased the item was satisfactorily mended.

At the back of our house in Link Road there was a vast area, several acres of scrubland, mostly sand. We used to play in this area. One day, Walter decided to dig a massive hole in the sand. He got into the hole, but suddenly the whole sand pit collapsed and completely buried him. It was a bit scary, because he was completely buried and Giles and I had to dig him out with our bare hands. Eventually we got him out, but if we hadn't been there, I don't know what would have happened. It was just one of the many things Walter got up to.

Dad taught me how to drive in Australia. Well, he showed me how he drove which wasn't really the correct way. He never had a civilian licence to drive. He was taught how to drive in the Army but never had an official licence. When I was eleven he let me drive our old truck for a few hundred yards on a dirt track. I didn't do so badly really although I was a bit too small to reach the pedals. My mother never learnt to drive, I think she was happy not to. I didn't travel much with Dad in the truck but there is one instance I will never forget. He was driving along with me next to him and he kept on putting his foot on and off the accelerator which made the car leap along the road like a kangaroo. I felt car sick. I made the mistake of asking him why he did it. He blew his top and started shouting at me. I don't know why, it was a perfectly reasonable question I thought. I didn't go with him again in the truck and kept my mouth shut. I learned to keep my mouth shut a lot in those days.

The house in Link Road was fairly modern although prefabricated. I once wondered how strong it was, I decided to test it. The cladding was so fragile I managed to put my fist through it and break a hole. There was quite a large pond at the back of the house and we would go and shoot mullet which were there. I don't know why we did it. We used an air rifle firing pellets and we managed to shoot and kill a couple of them. We would take it with us in the bush and kill snakes or other creatures. The owner of the house got a bit cross and told us not to do it. Sadly, while we lived at Link Road, the owner, a young chap, was killed in a water skiing accident.

While we lived at Link Road, I had an idea to write to the various embassies in Australia. It was to get information back about their country. I wrote

Me seated on left, with Giles, Mum and Walter.

to various ones saying I was interested in their country and I was doing a project at school about them (I wasn't). Anyway, all of the embassies I wrote to sent me a parcel of information with brochures and leaflets and so on. It was a real surprise. I wrote to as many as I could, just for the pleasure of getting a parcel every so often. I don't know where I got the idea from but it seemed to work. They were delighted someone took an interest in their country and were pleased to send me the information.

At Link Road, I started a club. I can't remember the name of the club, but it was for fighting with toy soldiers, and other objects. Quite a few of my friends came round actually. I thought it would be a good idea to charge them to 'join' the club. I charged them 6 old pence I think it was . Not a good idea, because they didn't come again. Oh well another good idea gone. I used to love playing with the toy soldiers.

Mum had an old typewriter which was a fully functional working model which we used but not in the conventional way. We used to put the plastic soldiers on the keys and press the relevant key letter to send them flying. It was great fun. We made the table into a fortress and banged small tacks into the wooden table to make a fence. Probably not a good idea, but both our parents didn't seem to mind us wrecking their table and their typewriter.

We had a dog called Flambo; a beautiful small collie puppy. He had to be locked in the garden for safety and we were very careful to always close the gate. However, one evening a friend of ours came round and when he left, he must have left the gate open. We didn't realise but Flambo had got out at night, and was run over by a car. The driver came to our door with the dog in his arms, quite distressed. Poor Flambo had only an hour or so to live. The vet came round after about half an hour and tried to do what he could, but in the end there was nothing he could do, so he put it out of its misery. Poor Flambo. This upset me very much, and I tried not to get angry with my friend who left the gate open. We didn't have another dog for a long time after wards.

Another day to remember or rather forget. We had a cat. The cat had kittens. Many of them. My mother decided to get rid of them in the only way she knew how: she drowned them. How did I know? There was a shed at the bottom of the garden at Link Road. For some reason, I happened to go into the shed. I saw these poor creatures kicking around trying to get out. I was only about ten. I was horrified and ran out. I daren't say anything. In fact, I never ever mentioned it to anyone but it did have a profound effect on my life. It was a truly horrible sight. I never want to witness anything like it ever again.

I found a tortoise once, on my way back from school. I was crossing a farmer's field as a shortcut and saw this tortoise in front of me. I was with a friend and took it home. However I gave it away to my friend for some reason. A few days later I asked for it back which he did. I kept the tortoise as a pet, gave it some food and built a netted cage for it outside. Unfortunately (for me) it must have burrowed underneath during the night and managed to 'run away'. When I looked at the cage the next morning it was gone and nowhere to be seen. I never did see it again.

Mosquitoes by this time never bothered me. They left me alone. I guess my blood had thinned and they just weren't bothered about biting me anymore. Maybe I had learned to live with them. They were still there, sometimes great swarms of them. In those days people would spray them using spray from small aircraft, but they would always come back. Sometimes the spray people would come round to the houses with mosquito sprayers on their backs and spray around the house.

I was very shy as a young boy and found it difficult to relate to some people. Especially girls. I thought they were strange creatures. I was rather fond of a couple of girls at school though and they seemed to like me. Paula Masters was one. She was a lovely girl with a good personality and liked talking to me. Another girl was Elizabeth Black. She was a very pretty brunette. I really liked her. I went to her birthday party once. My brothers and I were invited, surprisingly as we were never normally invited to anything. It was a good time and I think we got on socially, although as we arrived someone said, 'Oh no, not the Oldershaws', which didn't put me in a good frame of mind. Elizabeth started crying for some reason and sat down in the back of her Dad's car. As no one came to see her, I thought I would sit with her in the back and find out what was going on and try to comfort her. I'm not sure I succeeded but she eventually came out and rejoined the party. I grew very fond of her, but felt she was too good and too pretty for me.

Cleveland Yacht Club

Cleveland was a small town not far from Victoria Point. I joined a yacht club in Cleveland, although I didn't go to it very often. Once, when I did go, a yacht race about to start. I didn't know what was happening but I sat on a grassy hill watching the boats from a distance, with Mum and an older friend of mine. My friend told me to go up to the boats in the water. He said I would never get anywhere if I just sat on the sidelines waiting for things to happen. Rather reluctantly, I did what he said. I stood at the water's edge where the boats were and looked. I looked and felt like

Cleveland Yacht Club.

a prat actually. I looked at my friend on the side lines. He beckoned me to wade further into the water. I did. I felt even more foolish. The sea was up to my knees and I felt rather silly just standing there. There was a young guy about my age in a boat who asked if I wanted to go in the boat with him as he didn't have anyone to sail with. I said 'yes', and got in and we sailed this race. I was hopeless to be honest. I wasn't even aware it was a boat race. I kept on getting things wrong. If I was supposed to lean to the left, I leaned to the right and so on. The strange thing was, we won. (no thanks to me). I learnt a big lesson that day. You won't get anywhere in life if you just sit on the side lines. You need to get into the water. You need to get your feet wet and even to appear foolish. A valuable lesson for me in later life. I was still never good at sailing though.

One of my Dad's redeeming points was he was very generous, which is probably why he didn't have any money. If he had something and someone was in need he would give it away. Like our pick up truck. A young man wanted to borrow it to go out for the evening. In fact he borrowed it on many occasions and every time he brought it back on time. One evening it was different. My Dad said, 'Sure, you can borrow it', without question. He came back later that evening and rather sheepishly said, 'It rolled'. Not, 'I crashed the car and I am so sorry', but simply, 'It rolled' as if it was the car's fault. My Dad was very gracious and said, 'Oh, don't worry, it's alright'. There was never an apology, or an offer of money as compensation and my Dad just let it go. We never did get another car after this incident, we just didn't have the money. I don't know what happened to the car after the crash, I think it must have been scrapped. He could never hold on to money. He never saved. Although he can be commended for generosity, perhaps he should have thought about saving as well, to provide a future for themselves and for us children. Now, I think there has to be a balance with money. I believe in being generous but also being thrifty and saving. John Wesley once said, 'Earn all you can, save all you can, give all you can'.

Dad and Mum continued to work on the farms, going from one place to another looking for work. There was always farm work available. My

Dad would have been in his late fifties and Mum in her early forties. Dad was a bit work-shy, and would often turn up at a farm with his best suit on. My Dad would ask in his very posh English accent, 'Do you have any work at all?' After the farmer looked Dad up and down he would say, 'I am sorry Sir, but I'm afraid there is no work for you, we can't possibly give you a job'. Then next time he would turn up for an interview for an office job in his old raggy work clothes, and the manager would say the same thing. This was an attempt on Dad's part to not get employed. It seemed to work.

Dad was able to grow vegetables and we had a small plot where Dad grew runner beans, carrots and a few other vegetables. He was pretty good at gardening and I think I picked up my gardening skills from him.

School at this time was going on okay but I felt I wasn't learning anything. The state of my emotional and mental health were not good, with our constant moving about, difficulties relating to older parents, problems with Dad's temperament and trying to fit into a society which was so different to what I had been used to. In those early days, you didn't talk about where you came from. If you did there would be a name for you – 'Whinging Pom'. And there was a few of those about. Some of them were known as the 'Boomerang Pommies'. They would get fed up with Australia and after a couple of years go back to UK. But in the UK they would realise why they had left the UK in the first place, miss the sunshine and the easy going lifestyle of Australia. Then they would come back again as a £10 Pom. After a couple of years the pull of going back to UK was too great and off they would go again, and then repeat the cycle.

I began to love Australia. I loved the lifestyle and freedom and open air, the sunshine, beaches, fresh air. However, my parents were pining for a different lifestyle and I sensed an unease in them, a yearning for something else. They couldn't settle where they were. This greatly unsettled me and I felt pulled two ways. They were difficult times. I soon realised I had to integrate myself into the Australian way of life as soon as possible. If I didn't talk about England I would be okay and almost accepted. Almost. There was still hostility shown to me by some of the Aussie school children. Strangely enough they seemed to be okay with other nationalities who had migrated. There were a lot of Dutch children and I noticed they were treated very differently to me and my brothers - by the way, we were the only English immigrants in the school.

My parents didn't fit well into the Australian way of life. My Dad was Oxford educated and was a tutor of Classical Literature. There was hardly a need for it in the rural outback where we lived where it was all farming. All these things seemed to alienate us from the culture of Australia. However I tried hard to integrate myself into this lifestyle and I think I succeeded to some degree.

I think what affected me the most was the lack of consistency and the disruption in my life. Particularly the fact we moved ten times in as many years including several school moves and two countries.

It seemed as soon as I had made friends in one place we were on the move again to somewhere else. I don't know if it was a deliberate ploy on my Dad's part to disrupt us so much or, he fell out with the landlords or, he didn't like the place or he was just plain bored. They say you are either running away from something or running to something. I question my Dad's reasons. Whatever the reason I found this very disruptive and it affected me emotionally as well as educationally. There is no doubt a term now for my mental state as it was, but in those days there was no such thing as ADHD or any of the other types of disorders. You just got on with life. So, I did.

At Link Road I began to settle into the Australian way of life, and eventually really enjoyed it. I felt like an Aussie. I even got used to the school. I had made some good friends. We were now living in a relatively nice house and even had our own television. We were settling in at school. However the sense of belonging and the feeling of acceptance was not to last long. We would be on the move again and this move was to be the most disruptive for me, in every way. We left Australia in January 1966.

Chapter Thirteen

NEW ZEALAND

We were on the move again, we had already moved five times in Australia. This was one of the most challenging times of my life. We would be moving to New Zealand. Not just a local move this time, but to another country. We would be immigrants again. In our last few weeks of leaving, we said goodbye to our friends and school mates. It was the end of the school year and the beginning of the next. We said goodbye to our Aboriginal neighbours opposite who I particularly got on with, the Coolwells, especially Gwen and Elsie. I gave Elsie a badge with my name on it which she liked. All our furniture and possessions had been taken days before. I can't say I was going to miss the school, but I made some good friends there and I was beginning to feel settled. We left our Link Road home and travelled to Brisbane. We spent a good few hours in Brisbane, looking around the city and sitting in the park waiting for our train to Sydney.

I was really cross and upset about leaving. As far as I know my parents, as usual, never told us what was happening. 'How could you uproot us like this?' I thought. From Brisbane we travelled to Sydney by train and then by ship to Auckland. The train journey was very, very long. The train journey from Brisbane was about sixteen hours. We travelled all the way on hard seats. It was very uncomfortable. For hour after hour we would see nothing. And then occasionally we would see a house in the distance. Then after another couple of hours, nothing. Then another house. I tried to sleep but couldn't. We finally got to Sydney where we spent a few hours looking around. I was still cross and very upset.

When we went to the docks and boarded the ship, there was no one to see us off. No ceremony. No friends or relatives waving this time. No streamers.

The ship was called the Castle Felice, a sister ship of the Fairsky from the Sitmar Italian Line. We left on the 30th January 1966 travelled for just a few days. It was nice and relaxing and we enjoyed being looked after with three cooked meals a day. We had a good time although I was sea sick again for a day or two. We were a bit older now (15, 13 and 11) and didn't get involved in kid's games, but we were not old enough to participate in adult games. I wanted to have a go at clay pigeon shooting, but I wasn't allowed to. Didn't they know I used to own an air rifle in Australia? Too old for games and too young to go in the bar or enjoy adult activities. There wasn't a lot for us to do. We went to the cinema a few times. One of the movies we watched was *Dr Strangelove* which had just been released.

We travelled along the East Coast of New Zealand and arrived in Auckland with our bags. We had a look around the city. My parents had found a house in Devonport on the North Shore. A small town with one main street, lots of shops and a cinema. It was actually a very nice house; much better than the houses where we lived in Australia. It was close to the shops and schools. New Zealand didn't seem so bad after all. It was very different to Australia. We now had hot and cold running water which didn't come from rain tanks. The houses in the area were wooden and well built. There was even an inside toilet and a bathroom. Yet, there was not the same type of freedom to roam around as we did in Australia. Some of my Australian ways stuck with me though, like walking barefoot. I had also developed a bit of an Australian twang. Auckland city was just across the harbour, a few minutes ferry ride. We enjoyed going into the city and exploring our new surroundings. We had to get used to this new way of life and a very different culture to Australia. Strangely enough there didn't seem to be the discrimination I felt in Australia.

Walter (left) and Giles (right) larking about at Devonport Harbour

Things moved very quickly when we arrived. Mum found work as a clerical typist, but Dad still found it difficult to get work. We were soon enrolled in the local schools. I went to Devonport Primary. We were treated well in the school and weren't called Poms anymore. There was no corporal punishment in the schools either and the teachers were okay. However it wasn't all good. My education in Australia wasn't brilliant to say the least. The New Zealand school system didn't seem to recognise the Australian school system and so I was put back two years – the penultimate year of primary school with ten and eleven year olds. I was thirteen and I was really cross. Finally after much haranguing of education officials especially from Dad (which I thought was strange as up until now Dad didn't seem bothered about my education), I was reluctantly moved up a class by the authorities. I even had to take an IQ test to prove I was intellectually capable. I still think it was unfair. I was

Giles, Walter and Bob at Rotorua

still in a Primary school when I felt I should have started secondary. It meant I would always be nearly two years behind everyone else. This in itself made me bitter and angry for a long time. I was cross about leaving Australia, cross about living in New Zealand and cross about being put back educationally two years. It was a very tough time for me and mentally I was struggling. In fact, my mother said I cried every night for a whole year. Alone, in my bedroom, I felt the whole world was against me. I also started wetting the bed, which was highly embarrassing and difficult for me. This lasted a few years and caused me great anxiety.

I slowly started making friends and gradually was getting used to this new way of life. Some of them were the wrong type of friends and led me into a bit of trouble.

I needed to make some money and do part time jobs. My brothers and I went to the North Shore which was riddled with caves and old war hideouts. Left behind were copper wiring and solid brass window frames. I took them and sold them to a scrap metal merchant for about $40. It wasn't much considering how much we took. On one of our trips, with two heavy sacks full of brass and copper wire, we were careering down the road on a trolley when we almost crashed into a police car coming up the other way. The car stopped us, the policeman got out and asked us what we had in the sacks. We told him the truth: all we had was just a lot of old copper and brass. To which the policeman said, 'Okay, on your way then'. I also used to get copper wire from the local tip and melt it down in an oil drum fire in the back yard of our house. Our neighbours didn't like us doing it though as there were clouds of thick black smoke which ruined their washing. You could get more money for the copper wire if the plastic was melted off. I made a few dollars this way. We used to get lots of stuff from the tip. Stamps, books, copper, brass and electrical goods. All sorts really. It was surprising what people threw away. The man in charge used to chase after us if he knew we were about. We annoyed the 'dumpy man' as we called him.

I used to camp out at North Head from time to time with my friends. North Head is the area of coast around and to the east of Devonport. This was a beautiful area overlooking Auckland harbour, with a lovely long stretch of beach. It's a hilly area with lots of caves and disused war time bunkers. My friends and I would sometimes sleep in the caves dotted around the shore. They were a bit scary really, and went back quite a long way. We just camped out at the mouth of the caves, where it was reasonably dry. It would only be for a night during the summer. There were a number of old bomb shelters also, scattered around the top of the hill. Some of them were dangerous. Suddenly, as you were walking you could come across a big concrete shelter buried in the ground about 15 feet with no cover. My brother and I explored those shelters, and they were like big pits underground. There were stairs leading down. Then there were empty rooms leading off, all underground. I was surprised the council hadn't made it safe, even back then. Anyone could have fallen into one of those shelters and injured themselves. They were just abandoned.

Nowadays the whole area is vastly improved with parklands and walkways and seems to be a real tourist destination. I would love to go back sometime and see what it's like. I have not been back to New Zealand since leaving.

We soon settled in our new way of life and had to adapt again to the new culture. After a year, I moved up to the Grammar school along with my brother Walter who was in a class above.

The beaches in New Zealand were beautiful with long stretches of white sand. We often went swimming and I took up fishing again - I still didn't own a fishing rod but just had a hand line and still managed to catch a few fish, which I took home and Mum cooked them for us. Mum really liked this new culture especially as she didn't have to do back-breaking manual work of picking vegetables and fruit again. The job she had with the Naval Base as a clerical assistant really suited her and she passed several exams with her work. Dad still struggled to find work but eventually got a job in Auckland also as a clerical assistant but in a sorting office. He had

Mum at our first house in Devonport

to sort letters from all over the world and he would often bring me stamps from unusual places. I had taken up stamp collecting and was interested in all the different stamps.

Dad and Mum decided to go out for an evening. They were going to leave us alone for the first time. I was about fourteen or fifteen. Just us three looking after the house. What could go wrong? Well, a drunk came to the house knocking on our door. We opened the door and before we could say anything he pushed past us and let himself in and sat down in one of the chairs. He was muttering and mumbling away about everything and anything. He wasn't violent but he seemed unpredictable. I was scared. I decided to go to the nearest phone box and ring for the police. I dialled the number but it didn't ring. I tried again and again but no response. So I went back home. Fortunately, Walter had taken the matter in his own hands and he called one of the neighbours who came round and managed to escort the man off the premises. I think Mum and Dad were a bit shocked when they came back from their night out. It was a long time before they went out again.

We stayed in Devonport for about a year, and we all got settled in our new way of life. Walter, Giles and I had eventually got settled in our new schools and enjoying learning. However, it was not long before we were going to move again, such was the pattern of our lives.

Chapter Fourteen

GREENHITHE

Our first move in New Zealand was from Devonport to Milford just a few miles away. We only stayed there a few weeks for some reason. We quite liked it there though; it was close to shops and a church which I started going to. I really enjoyed going to the Church in Milford. But we weren't there for long and we were on the move again. This time our move was to Greenhithe, a small village just a few miles away.

Greenhithe was a nice quiet little village. Just a few houses at the time but a little out of the way. It was mostly farmland with a very small population. To go anywhere you had to rely on a bus, but there weren't any in Greenhithe itself. If you didn't have transport you either had to walk to the nearest main road which was about three miles away, or catch a taxi. We three boys had to get a local taxi to the main road to get the school bus to Westlake Boy's High School. Giles and Walter went on to Takapuna Grammar. For some reason, Mum moved us all out of the Grammar school to Westlake Boys, but Giles and Walter didn't like it and so went back to the Grammar school. I think I was past caring and stayed at Westlake. We got moved around so much and I just wanted to settle down. I made a few friends at Westlake: John Harrop was one. I used to go to his house sometimes at lunchtime and sit down and have lunch with him. He only lived a few minutes' walk away He was a Christian and I had good chats with him. We were later to go hitchhiking around New Zealand together with another friend, Don Hounsell.

Decimilisation seemed to follow us. Not long after we arrived, New Zealand went decimal and so we got used to the new currency again.

Westlake Boys' High

I didn't particularly enjoy Westlake and I don't think I learnt much there really, at least initially. Once, I skipped a Maths class by hiding in the toilet. I don't think the teacher even noticed I was missing. I hated Maths or perhaps I hated the way it was being taught. I liked the English class. Mainly because there was a beautiful woman teacher who taught us, and wore short skirts. I don't think any of the boys could concentrate on what she was teaching. I remember we were asked to write about a topic and then present it to the class. I wrote about cyclamates (food additives). I think I was ahead of my time because in years to come it was to be a very important subject. I remember talking to the class. Being very nervous and shy I wasn't very confident in my delivery. The teacher was half listening as she was going round the class marking books. She did say at the end of my talk that she really enjoyed it, said it was really important and she wished she could have sat down and listened properly to what I was saying. This encouraged me and helped me to gain more confidence.

There was also a geography teacher who I really liked. He used to go on about the war, and regaled us with his war stories. He was easily distracted and loved to talk, and I used to like listening to him. I enjoyed his lessons immensely. He made geography, which can be a bit boring, come alive and interesting. He was an older man and his stories were really interesting. I felt relaxed in his class which seemed to really help me to learn. I also enjoyed art. The art teacher was very laid back, and would always write on my report, 'learning and improving'. He just let us loose on whatever we wanted to do, and would come round occasionally to see what we were doing. Even though it was a bit of a free for all I enjoyed it. His style of teaching obviously suited me.

I joined a tennis club at Westlake. I had some lessons and enjoyed it very much. We played a few matches, but unfortunately I wasn't very good although I did try. Dad bought me a tennis racket; I played all the time and practised at home. It was the only sport I played as I wasn't particularly good at sports especially team sports. I played tennis with Dad on a couple of occasions. There were some tennis courts in the village and I could practice there. Although Dad was getting on a bit, he would have been in his sixties, he got me running round the court like crazy. He always beat me at tennis he was such a good player, despite his age.

After a year, I progressed to the fifth form which was School Certificate year. Once you passed the New Zealand School Certificate you could either leave school or stay on in the sixth form for two more years. I studied reasonably hard for the exams but I did find it a bit of a struggle. I think there was too much going on in my life for me to concentrate on my studies. When the time came to take the exams, I thought I had done enough studying and revising to get me through. I was nervous and a little unprepared. After finishing the exams there was the long wait of a few weeks before we got the results. The day came when I found out what I had achieved. I didn't pass. I was devastated. I failed the New Zealand School Certificate by five marks. You had to get 50% in four subjects to pass and go on to the sixth form. It was annoying for me as it meant I had to do a retake if I wanted any sort of qualifications. I was so cross. I was already about two years behind the rest of my classmates anyway. I had to take the whole year again. The upside was I was pretty good at the subjects by then. I found myself in a class called '5 Senior A' along with a lot of other students who hadn't passed. I did pass the second time and got my school certificate, but it was still a close thing. I lacked a lot of confidence generally but at school in particular. However somehow I seemed to relate well with my classmates and they respected me. I'm not sure quite why as I was so full of self-doubt. I was never bullied at any

New Zealand school, unlike in Australia. I got on well with most of the teachers even though I didn't do so well academically and struggled. I believe I was reasonably intelligent but all the moving about and upheaval in my life wasn't conducive to learning.

We were all growing up and doing our own things. Walter had a few girlfriends he went out with. I don't think he was serious with any of them and I don't think he had any girl friends for long. I was a bit envious of him because I was so shy I felt I couldn't go out with anyone. I was almost too scared to talk to girls at the time. I used to think they were strange people, but nevertheless really liked them. I became friends with a guy called Stuart McMonagle. He really did like the girls. We were on the beach with one of the local girls and he said 'I'll show you mine if you show me yours'. She was wearing a skimpy bikini. Thankfully she had the good sense not to. As far as that went I was completely naïve. I didn't really know what a girl had underneath her bikini. I had no idea. At the time I was keen to find out though. But I was too shy, way too shy.

I continued to enjoy listening to the many pop songs coming out at the time. Songs like *Hey Jude* by The Beatles in 1968 and songs by Johnny Cash and Bob Dylan. The Rolling Stones were becoming very successful, although I was never really keen on their music. But it was a great period of time musically and then flower power came in and the whole hippie movement began, especially since the release of Scott Mackenzie's song, *San Francisco*. The Woodstock Festival happened in 1969 which seemed to be a defining moment and although I didn't see much of it on TV I felt I was a part of this whole culture of emerging pop music.

The moon landing happened when we were living in Greenhithe. This was on July 20th, 1969. I remember it well as we watched it on a black and white TV at Stuart McMonagles. For some reason we didn't have a TV then, I'm not sure why. We all sat on their settee and watched in amazement as Neil Armstrong coming out of Apollo 11 and landing on the moon. It was an incredible sight. I was amazed at the fact that two people were walking on the moon. And when Neil Armstrong famously said, 'It's one small step for man, one giant leap for mankind', it was really a moment in history. It was mind-blowing to see it live.

For a time, I was a member of the St John Ambulance Brigade, along with my two brothers. We really enjoyed being a part of the organisation. We would go to the meetings and learn all about First Aid. We would learn what to do in an emergency or if someone wasn't breathing. We learnt about bandages and how to apply those bandages to various parts of the body. We even had our own uniform. Walter had a special uniform because he was promoted to something or other. We could collect badges as well for doing things like hiking, or rescuing someone, or resuscitating them. I got a few of them because I liked collecting badges and certificates. We went on a hike one time for a couple of days. There was this camp leader who chain smoked. Literally, as soon as he finished one cigarette he lit up another. He must have been very nervous. We had a family photo taken of all us when we were at Greenhithe. We never bought the large photos but we were allowed to keep the smaller photos because they were free. I often went to special courses in Auckland to further enhance my skills.

Bob, Walter and Giles - St. John Ambulance Brigade

We had a dog in Greenhithe. A black Labrador which was a rescue dog. I think it had been hit by a car at some point. It was a lovely natured dog and we loved it. One day as were going to catch the bus via the lady taxi driver she mentioned a dog had ravaged her chickens during the night and killed some of them. During the next few days she said the same thing happened. Other people also had had chickens killed. Did we know what animal did it and whose it was? I didn't have a clue. However, over the next few weeks, we discovered what had been killing the chickens. It was our lovely dog. For some reason, at night time it had a blood lust and went weird. Unfortunately and reluctantly we had to put the dog down. It was heartbreaking for me as I really loved our dog. Very sad.

I caught the flu while we were living at Greenhithe. The year was 1968. The flu was known as the 1968 flu pandemic, also called Hong Kong Flu pandemic of 1968 or Hong Kong Flu of 1968. It originated in China in July 1968 and lasted until 1969–70. It was highly contagious and spread globally. The death toll of the pandemic was immense; estimated between one million and four million deaths. Thankfully, I was not one of them, but I think I came close. I was in bed with it for nearly two weeks with a very high temperature. No one came in to see me during the day except Mum who would come in to see me for a few minutes after she finished work. I was completely bed bound. She came in with a mask on, and she would spray fly spray in the room before she came in. Why she did this I don't know, presumably to kill off any bugs. I was very lonely and miserable during those days. I got over it eventually and went back to school. But it left me very weak and tired.

Dad and I would often play chess together. It was a bit of a one sided affair with Dad always winning. Well, nearly always. I wrote in my diary that I beat Dad once. Which was pretty good going, as Dad seemed to play chess nearly every day of the week. He would play by himself, but obviously preferably with someone else. Giles and Walter hardly ever played with him, I don't think they liked chess at all. It seemed to me to be a very time consuming hobby really. He also liked to do crosswords, and again there was never a day I don't think when he wasn't pondering over some crossword puzzle. I think it kept his mind active which was a good thing. On the downside, he became disassociated with other things, like family life, which possibly wasn't so good.

Dad was quite a self absorbed man. I think he liked his own company, or at least he liked it a little better than other people's company. In later life, back in the UK, he used to play chess with a young man called Mike Pearson. I think he was a friend of Walter's, initially. A university graduate, he became a gardener tending the gardens at Oxford College.

Our house in Greenhithe was the last place we lived in as a family, as Walter and Dad went back to UK in 1970.

Chapter Fifteen

PROBLEMS AT HOME

Being constantly on the move definitely had an effect on my emotional and mental health. Mental health issues in those days were not really discussed in school. You just got on with it. There didn't seem to be the support then as there is nowadays. Also, what had caused me great anxiety was Dad's temperament which was becoming more and more erratic. One day he could be pleasant and nice, another day he could shout and scream and throw things around the room. There was the time when we were living in Devonport and he had just got a job and he wanted to celebrate. We were having dinner around the table like we always did and he had bought a bottle of red wine which he wanted to share with us kids. I was still only thirteen at the time. Mum thought we boys were too young to drink alcohol and said, 'No, Peter don't give them any, they're too young to have any.' Dad insisted anyway. 'Oh let the boys have some' he said. Mum kept on saying 'No, you shouldn't give them any'. As Mum became more insistent, Dad got madder and madder, until he exploded and threw everything around the room - all the dinner plates with food on it, the side board with all the china, he smashed every single plate. Then he stormed off. In a way I don't blame him, perhaps Mum could have responded better than she did. Maybe she should have complied and allowed Dad to give us a glass of wine. But this sure left us traumatised. I mean what do you do after that?

This was just one of many episodes of Dad's anger coming out. The problem was one never knew when he was going to react. Another time, in New Zealand, a friend of Walter's had come round to the house to see him. Dad beckoned him in. Dad then proceeded to offer him a seat to sit down. 'Oh do sit down', he said in his posh Oxford accent. 'Nah, it's alright mate', he responded, in his broad New Zealand accent. This refusal alone would have riled my father who insisted everyone spoke the Queen's English. 'Oh please do take a seat', my father said again, slightly more impatiently. 'Nah, it's alright mate', he replied again. My father exploded shouting and screaming at him, with spit dribbling from his mouth. 'You sit down when I tell you to. Do you understand?' The poor lad didn't know what hit him. He ran out of the house and never came back. Dad went to his room to calm down. After this episode no one ever came round to the house. Dad would often get upset like this for no apparent reason. You didn't know when he would become aggressive, which was the problem. One minute he could be all calm and polite, the next he would explode in uncontrollable outbursts. We were walking on eggshells a lot of the time. I think his anger was borne out of immense frustration in his life. I'm sure he realised what he was like. He couldn't hold down a proper job, he wasn't successful in his career, he had money worries, he felt isolated and alone and had failed academically. The list goes on.

Living with an unpredictable father, living in an unfamiliar country with a different culture and the difficulties of just growing up was extremely difficult for a thirteen year old.

Very often if I did something or said something he disagreed with he would say 'fool'. Even when playing chess with him, if I made an incorrect move he would say something negative. Needless to say, I didn't play too much chess with him. He could never bring himself to say anything positive about me or anyone else for that matter. He would criticise certain people on the television or he would criticise his colleagues and find fault with them. I can't remember him saying anything good about anyone. It was sad really. It didn't help my confidence levels and it took me years to disassemble these negative thoughts and feelings I had.

Being very sensitive I took all these things on board and it dramatically affected my confidence. It didn't matter if other people were positive about me, I just focused on the negative things Dad would say. He didn't like it if he thought people were better than him, he had real issues. He also had mental health issues and seemed to be dogged by troubles all his life. It never really seemed to lift from him. I think his behaviour was the result of being in the Army, which he never, or rarely, talked about. He suffered nightmares all his life.

He had little jokey sayings like, 'Some say "Good old Bobby"....others tell the truth. Ha ha ha!' This would have been from my early childhood days, when I was very impressionable. I don't know what he was thinking, but he never really had a good word to say, he would always say something to upskittle me. He never said 'I love you', for instance. I think he was jealous of people's success, especially of his brothers and sisters who were all more successful than he was – they all had good successful careers. Dad was known as the black sheep of the family – for many reasons. Dad just couldn't bring himself to say good positive things. This created in me a bit of a resentment.

I started to rebel against my Dad and would react to his comments. The atmosphere at home wasn't good, generally. Mum was always having a go at Dad for something or other. Usually for not pulling his weight around the house, like cleaning up and so on. Mum was the main breadwinner and would come in from a hard day's work, had to catch two buses to do so and would get back about 6.30pm. Then, she would cook a meal and very often wash up too. Sometimes I would help and I think my brothers did too. I think she felt it was her duty. Mum seemed to do everything. Go out to work, do the cooking, washing up after dinner, cleaning, ironing, even the decorating. There were often shouting matches between her and Dad and a we felt a lot of tension over it. Yet, they seemed to love each other. I think Mum made life more difficult for herself by never insisting we help with the small domestic chores, but she did complain about it.

Dad didn't seem too bothered about the state of the house. He would often sit around a lot of the day, doing crosswords, playing patience or chess, or reading a books. Dad also liked playing croquet and he taught us how to play. I really enjoyed playing this with him and despite his dourness at times he had a good sense of humour, usually at other people's expense. He once told a very large lady who came to the door, 'Oh do come in. Have a seat. Have two.' Or as he said to another person who had come for a visit, 'Must you stay can't you go.' Or another phrase he used on a person - 'I'd like to help you out, which way did you come in?' He could be quite embarrassing at times.

Another time when Walter was in a restaurant with Dad, Dad had put some paper and bits and pieces in an ash tray on the table and set light to it. Flames suddenly shot up and other diners were somewhat alarmed. A waiter came and he was escorted off the premises. It didn't seem to bother him though, as he seemed to think he could do or say anything. He was in a shop waiting to be assisted by a bored sales assistant. After several moments, the assistant rather laconically drawled 'Can I help you?' to which my father replied, in his slow and deliberate Oxford accent, 'I don't think so', and walked out.

My childhood problems became exacerbated in later life and my mental health suffered. I grew up with an inferiority complex and thought everyone was better than me and that something was wrong with me. I wasn't like everyone else. I was different.

Chapter Sixteen

BECOMING A CHRISTIAN IN NEW ZEALAND

I was at a very low point, emotionally and physically really. I wasn't happy in my first year of being in New Zealand. I was depressed and longed to go back to Australia. I couldn't seem to adjust to this new way of life. Towards the end of the first year though something happened to me which would change the course of my life forever. I became a Christian. It seemed God hadn't forgotten me after all. It all started when Mum had seen an advert in the Auckland Herald for a week's holiday at a camp in Dargaville. This was for school children to go on a camp during the summer holidays. Before we went on the camp, Mum wanted to speak to the organiser, whose name was Peter Plummer. He came round to our house in Devonport and I think from the conversations Mum had with him she must have been reassured it wasn't some sort of religious cult or anything as she had noticed, in an advert for the camp, a Bible was listed as one of the essential things to bring. She thought it was a bit strange. I think she was glad for us boys to go away for a week so she could have a bit of a rest from us. I had turned fourteen, but I was a bit apprehensive about the camp as my previous experience with religious camps in Australia wasn't good and I had said to myself I wouldn't go on another 'religious' camp. The camp was for boys and girls, though the girls would attend in a different week. It was full on with activities every day and during the evening. I think what really spoke to me the most was the journey up to Dargaville on the coach. It was a long journey and took several hours. Everyone, at least all the adults, on the bus seemed so nice and friendly. I hadn't really experienced this before. People seemed to be genuinely interested in me. But neither did they 'bible bash' me either. I was half expecting they might, after all it was a religious event. But no, they were just normal, nice people. When we arrived we got settled in to the camp. It was a bit like a military operation with lots of rules and regulations. I was a bit nervous.

The owner of the camp, Graham Crawshaw came out to greet us. He was a great guy, very down to earth and a man's man. He was a dairy farmer and had a number of sheep and cattle which he looked after. The leader of the camp, Peter Plummer, was the main driving force behind the camps though with help from other adult leaders, including at times from his brothers, Richard and Doug. They must have seen many hundreds go through the camps and learn about Jesus. I went to many more camps after the first one, but my brothers never went back. Peter told us the rules and showed us where we would be sleeping – in corrugated tin huts on hard wooden beds with a thin mattress. Not exactly five star, but I'd slept in worse.

I was starving and we soon sat down to a hearty meal, cooked by a wonderful chef by the name of Jack. Jack was an interesting guy, an older man in his early 50s I would say, although to me anyone over 30 was old. He spoke on the first night to forty children in a little room at the top of the barn. He had been in the Navy and had become a hardened drinker. He gave his 'testimony', a short talk on how he had become a Christian. He explained in simple terms how he had become a Christian and he had seven demons in him, from which he was delivered. I didn't know what it really meant but he was the most sincere man I have ever heard. He sang a solo – *I'd rather have Jesus* by Rhea F Miller and George Beverly Shea.

This almost brought me to tears, because he meant every word of it. It was a song he would sing at every camp meeting.

I'd rather have Jesus than silver or gold
I'd rather be His than have riches untold
I'd rather have Jesus than houses or land
I'd rather be led by His nail-pierced hand
Than to be the king of a vast domain
And be held in sin's dread sway
I'd rather have Jesus than anything
This world affords today

He told us how he had become a Christian and how the experience had changed his life. A sincere man, Jack had little possessions or money. He seemed to live hand to mouth. But he had everything. He had life in all its abundance. He was happy.

Straight after his talk, I heard the gospel for the first time in my life. In Christian language the 'gospel' means good news. A man called Ben Siaki spoke. He was a Pastor from the Cook Islands and told us in his preaching how we were all going one way and we needed to 'repent' which means turn around and go the other way, to turn back to God. The only way to do this was to ask Jesus into our lives. It made sense to me, even as a fourteen year old. So when the preacher asked if anyone would like to ask Jesus into their lives I put up my hand. Little did I know, my two brothers also put their hands up. I didn't know it at the time and only found out many years later. In fact, my older brother Walter became a Christian in Banbury in the 1970s when we had come back to England. But that's another story.

My week on the camp was not without incident though. As I was sitting down on one of the benches at the meal table, I got up and the long wooden bench fell down on my bare foot – I nearly always went barefoot especially when I was in Australia, but even when we lived in New Zealand. I cut my foot badly and there was a two-inch gash with blood everywhere. Graham drove me to the nearest hospital, in Dargaville. As my foot was being stitched Graham told me some stories which diverted my attention from the pain. My foot was in a bandage and I couldn't walk on it very much. I just had to hobble along. Back at camp, the following day we were due to go on a hike for a few miles. Graham Braddock, one of the leaders lifted me up on his back and carried me all the way and back again. His genuine concern for my well-being really spoke to me and convinced me Christianity was real by the love which was shown to me. He told me a story from the Bible which has stayed with me to this day. It was the story of the sower who went out to sow. Some seed fell on stony ground some fell on weeds and some fell on good ground. He explained the seed was the word of God and that the seed which fell on stony ground was like the word of God that was given to people who refused to listen. The seed that fell amongst weeds was like seed that

At Arapohue Bush Camp, New Zealand. Me, Back row, second from left.

initially grew, but the cares of this world and other things got in the way and choked the word that had been planted. And the seed which fell on good ground was like the word that was given to people who listened and responded and it bore fruit in their lives. (Matthew 13: 1-33). This message stayed with me and I was determined to be the good seed on good ground.

So life changed for me a bit after camp. I was helped along the way by lots of people, I started going to Church and reading the Bible which I found really helpful. I had a bet with a friend I had made at the camp that we would read the Bible cover to cover over the summer holidays. We would get a prize for the first one who did it. I read the Bible through cover to cover over the summer holidays. I loved reading it. We didn't

Me, outside one of the tin huts I helped to build.

have a Bible at home as far as I knew, but I won a Bible in a competition at the camp. Apparently my friend was the first to finish or so he said. But I actually doubt it as he was full of bravado, but who knows. I wasn't going to argue and at least he read it. Unfortunately, I later learned he went off the rails and joined the Hells Angels and I lost touch with him.

I was very intense as a young man and took my Christianity very seriously. It was a big change for me. My parents didn't go to church, although my mother was quite 'religious'. Dad appeared to be a bit of an agnostic, but he had had a lot of Christian influence in his younger days. My life was turned upside down. Dad wasn't antagonistic about me becoming a Christian but wasn't exactly supportive either. Mum seemed concerned.

Becoming a Christian at Arapohue Bush Camp certainly changed my life. There were no flashing lights or anything and initially nothing dramatic really happened. Nothing miraculous. I didn't even feel anything particularly, but I had a strange sense of peace and the feeling all was well. I seemed connected to God and was able to speak to Him for the first time. I changed in a number of ways. I no longer went out with some of my more undesirable friends. I had a hunger to read the Bible, and I couldn't get enough of reading it. I went round to Peter Plummer's house quite a lot of weekends. He was just newly married and the leader of the camps. They were formative times for me and it really helped me at the time.

During the early years of being in New Zealand I would try and get to Church, meet other Christians and go to Peter Plummer's house. Occasionally, I would stay the weekend and go to his Church in Auckland city centre. The Church was a small room above a department store called Menzies. There were only about twenty people attending. We would sing a few songs and Peter would preach. Sometimes when I called in to Peter's house he would be in but not always. I couldn't contact him to tell him I was coming as he didn't have a 'phone. In those days we didn't have the luxury of mobile phones, or even telephones in the house. If someone didn't have access to a phone at all, it was difficult to reach them. I enjoyed Peter's company and he helped me spiritually. Peter was a big character, an extrovert larger than life.

I usually sat in Peter's living room listening to old tapes by a man called Willie Mullen for hours. Peter wanted to mentor me, and took me on a Christian correspondence course.

So I would go to Peter's house for the weekend and go to Church and then somehow get the bus back to Greenhithe where we lived at the time. I learnt a lot from our meetings and I went for about two or three years. When I stopped going, I went to a local church but it was a difficult as we often lived miles away from anywhere.

He took me through a Bible study course, and really helped me as a young Christian. Peter and his wife were a young couple, but at the time I didn't fully appreciate the fact they needed time to be alone together.

One time I went to a couple's house in the Dargaville region. It was a work party for the Christian couple and quite a few of us were there including my friend Paul, who I travelled with. We were doing the house up and I was painting and decorating which I thoroughly enjoyed. We ate well and the owner showed us some of us the fish he had caught. It was quite ingenious how he caught them, which was with a large fishing net along the shore line. It was offshore fishing. He arranged the nets in such a way so the fish could swim in but they couldn't find the way out so when the tide went out a great shoal of fish would be floundering in just a few inches of water. Genius I thought. We were there for a long weekend. On the last day we were given a meal which was cooked outside. The meal of lamb and vegetables was placed on a large metal tray with wet tea towels on top and wrapped up. Then it was placed on hot coals in a hole in the ground about three feet deep. Next it was covered with earth while we waited a few hours for it to be cooked. This was called a Hāngī, a traditional Maori method of cooking. Different types of food could be prepared such as fish and kumara (sweet potato), as well as meat and cooked in a pit dug in the ground. A Hāngī was traditionally wrapped in flax leaves; a modern Hāngī is more likely to use mutton cloth, wet tea towels or aluminium foil. The Hāngī is left in the ground for about three to four hours, depending on the amount of food. The result of this process is tender meat and delicious vegetables, infused with smoky, earthy flavours. The traditional Maori Hāngī (earth oven) is a centuries-old cooking method used to feed a crowd of hungry people and bring the community together. It certainly did for us. There were about ten of us and we all enjoyed the food as it was brought out. It had a smoky succulent flavour which you don't get when cooking in an oven. It was very delicious. I never had a Hāngī again after that. I don't think Mum would have been too pleased if I had dug a hole in the ground and buried food.

I had to make my own way as a Christian with the help of some good friends. The questions I had been asking myself all those years ago like 'Who am I?',' What am I doing here?', 'What is my life all about?' were being answered as I read the Bible. Somehow everything all seemed to make sense. The more I read the Bible the better life became for me. When I prayed my prayers seemed to be answered. Even my relationship with Dad changed, I was no longer antagonistic toward him.

I went on a number of Christian Camps at Arapohue over the next few years. One time when I went as a leader, I was only about 16. I was going to be leading a group of much younger boys aged about nine or ten years old. Anyway as we got off the coach and waiting for our luggage, the driver hauled out a big suitcase with 'Oldershaw' on the label clearly visible to everyone. As he chucked it on the ground out fell a couple of porn magazines. (I was horrified!) Walter had offered to carry my case to the coach – a suspicion of 'sabotage' was forming in my head. I didn't know where to put myself. One of the senior leaders picked up the magazines, looked at them and said, 'Disgusting'. This was very embarrassing for me as all eyes were on me. I don't know what people thought. Unbeknown to me my brothers had rigged the suitcase so the the magazines they'd put inside at the top would fall out at the slightest impact. I was really annoyed at them. Later, my brothers thought it was a great laugh but I was hugely embarrassed at the time.

I would often go as a leader to groups of lads at Arapohue. We did various activities every day and we were always outside during the day often walking for miles. One day we had a picnic in the pine forest and then a swim in the dam. There was a zip line into the dam which I went on. It was a bit scary and dangerous and there were no health and safety legislations as there are now. The zip line went from the top of a hill straight into and over the dam. No one got hurt fortunately. At least not as far as I know. One time I went horse riding. It wasn't really a lesson and looking back, it was quite dangerous. I got on a horse bareback and it suddenly bolted off down a hill until it could go no further because of a fence. So it galloped back up the hill and was tried to throw me off. Fortunately, I stayed on and it eventually came to a stop. It was scary.

On another week at the camp I helped build one or two of the huts. It was a working week and I learnt how to construct a building with corrugated iron. First the frame went up and then large corrugated steel sheets were nailed to it. It was very easy really and only took us two or three days to construct each one. We also made the timber framed bunk beds.

During the week, we watched slides and saw films, read stories and listened to various speakers. I really liked the films which usually showed how someone's life had been changed by becoming a Christian. I often went fishing and had a swim in a local creek where we would catch fish and eels for supper.

Another embarrassing time for me at the boy's camp was in a meeting of about forty children. Peter suddenly asked me to say a few words, give my 'testimony' in front of everyone. I froze. I was stood in front of so many kids and I didn't know what to say. 'Umm, err, well I' and so on. After a few embarrassing seconds Peter put me out of my misery and I sat down. It wasn't a good time and I cringe even now thinking about it. I was so self-conscious in those days and terrified of public speaking. But Peter really helped me in my early days and I slowly gained confidence.

Not long after I became a Christian I got baptised. I remember it well. It was in a Chinese Church in Auckland. It was led by Ben Siaki the Fijian pastor, who was the pastor at the Church Camp in Dargaville, the person who helped me to become a Christian. I had to give my 'testimony' in front of hundreds, and it was a bit nerve racking, but I held my nerve and did well. My parents who came with me and saw me being baptised didn't say much about it on the journey home. I'm not sure what was going through their minds at the time. Becoming a Christian radically changed my life. I was a new person, I thought differently and acted differently. It took me a while to readjust to this way of life, and I think it may be why people must have thought I was a bit strange. I was also adjusting to growing pains at the time, and adjusting to hormones and peer pressure and generally life at that age. But I knew I was different somehow. Becoming a Christian for me was the best thing I ever did. I had some new Christian friends I had made at the High School and one summer went hitch-hiking around New Zealand with a couple of them.

Chapter Seventeen

MY HITCHHIKING ADVENTURE

My two friends (John Horrop and Don Hounsell) and I left Devonport and the plan was to hitch-hike around the North Island, south of Auckland. We had very little money on us, just a rucksack and nothing much else. We didn't even have a map. We had no particular plan, just 'Where the Spirit led us'. My two friends were Pentecostal Christians, I was a type of very reserved brethren. We were a mixed bunch, but we got on well together. We started hitch-hiking and we got pretty good lifts with some amazing people. We travelled down to Lake Taupo in the middle of the North Island and looked at the lake there. It took us a day and we were able to look around the sides of the very large lake, in fact the largest fresh water lake in New Zealand. We slept where we could, on wooden benches in the open the first night. We then set off for Napier on the eastern side of the island. We really didn't know where we were heading, we just seemed to follow our instincts. We were totally unprepared. We got a lift but the route there was treacherous across the mountain ranges. The bends were hair-raising and as I looked down the gorges, I saw cars which hadn't made it. The roads at times were almost single track, but it didn't seem to bother our driver who apparently could see round bends doing more than 60mph. Somehow we finally got to the city called Napier. We thanked the driver as we hurried out of the car. Napier is a beachside city on the east coast. After a look around we headed to an Anglican Church and happened to meet the Vicar. He asked us about ourselves and where we were staying the night and we said we were sleeping on the beach. We left and went on our way, taking in the sights of this beautiful city and having a bite to eat at a local café. As evening drew near we decided to camp out on the beach and sleep under the stars. We didn't have a tent, just a sleeping bag. Before we settled down we heard someone coming. It was the vicar, and he had come to invite us into his house. He must have had a chat to his wife and they both agreed we could stay the night. It was very generous of them; not many people would entertain three young men who they'd never met before. We had a good night's sleep followed by an excellent breakfast. We thanked the vicar and his wife for their generosity and set off on our journey again.

A North Island town we passed through

This time we were travelling down south. We got to one small town and we stood at a cross roads. We didn't know where to go. It was a literal and a metaphorical crossroads. We didn't know where to turn. We were a bit fed up and despondent at this stage. We were hungry with nowhere to sleep that night and it was early evening with the light fading. I suddenly had an inspiration and said 'I will be back in a minute'. I didn't know what I was going to do, but I walked up a bit further and went round a bend. Suddenly I saw a sign which said 'Riverbend Christian Youth Camp'. Brilliant I thought. I raced back to the others and said 'Follow me!' My friends were totally surprised and we saw it as an answer to prayer. We went in and saw the manager. He said they were closed for the season. Our faces dropped.

'However', he said, 'I can let you in and you can stay for however long you like'.

'Great!' we said. 'We haven't got much money though.' 'No problem, I will fix you up with work with a local farmer,' he replied and he did. The next day, we started peach thinning for a farmer who had hundreds of peach trees. I've never done peach thinning before (or since) but basically you prune the tree of extra peaches so the peaches which are left can grow bigger. Peaches grow in clusters and to get a fully ripe peach you have to break off its neighbours. There might be four or five in a cluster. It was tiring work, but we got paid well and it enabled us to stay at the camp and eat well. We were able to wash our clothes as well as shower ourselves as we hadn't washed for several days.

We went to the local town on the Sunday and decided to look for a Church. I said I would look for a Brethren church and my two friends said they would look for a Pentecostal church. Brethren Churches aren't noted for their spontaneity or freedom in worship but it seemed to suit me at the time. Pentecostal or Charismatic Churches on the other hand are very much noted for their lively 'happy clappy' worship. We agreed to meet up afterwards. As it happened, I found a church which looked suitably boring and went in. I was greeted by a small boy who looked about five years old. No one else spoke to me. They sat round in a circle and spoke in 'tongues' for most of the service interjected by a few hymns and a bit of reading. (Speaking in Tongues is a New Testament term and is a sign of someone receiving the Holy Spirit; it's often known as a 'heavenly language'). The whole service was very freaky. This went on for an hour or so. It didn't make any sense whatsoever to me and as I left no one said goodbye or even acknowledged me – except the five year old boy who said 'Goodbye'. It was the weirdest church I have ever been into. I got outside and my two friends were already outside the Church waiting for me.

It transpired the church they thought was charismatic was in fact a brethren Church. There you go, appearances can be deceptive. We started walking home; it was early evening with the light fading when suddenly, out of nowhere, we were set upon by a small gang of youths,

The two friends with whom I hitch-hiked. Don (left) and John (right)

probably about eight of them. They started hitting my friends and punching them to the ground. Why, I don't know. My two friends and I were slightly separated from each other at this point and the youths concentrated on hitting my friends and ignoring me for some reason. Anyway my friends got up and managed to get away from the group. Which left me by myself. 'Here we go', I thought. Miraculously, they said 'make sure your friends don't do that again' which was decidedly odd as we'd had no previous dealings with them. I said, 'Sure', and walked straight on past them whilst they moved away. They didn't touch me. Did they see angels? Why didn't they beat me up? I don't know, but I believe it was God's protection.

After two weeks we left Riverbend Christian Youth Camp and hitch-hiked home. We agreed we would split up and hitch-hike separately as we would get more of a chance of getting a lift. Why we hadn't thought of it before I don't know. I got lifts with various people. I had to travel the treacherous route back from Napier to Lake Taupo again and as it happened I got a lift with a crazy driver. He didn't take the bends very carefully but sped around them like he was in a race. I thought any moment a car will be coming the other way and that would be it. I looked out of the window and I could see the sheer drop below, some hundreds of feet. He drove like there was no one else on the road and no tomorrow! I was very relieved when he dropped me off in Lake Taupo.

I managed to get several lifts but none of them long distance. I was doing very well until the last lift to Auckland. Unfortunately, it was with a drunk driver. I should have got out of the car, but I was young and scared. Instead of dropping me off in Auckland city centre, he insisted on taking me to his house in one of the suburbs of Auckland to meet the 'Missus'. I didn't know what to expect. Anyway we got in and actually it wasn't too bad, he was just really drunk. I did meet 'the missus' who wasn't overly impressed by her drunken husband. I felt compelled to stay for a while, after all he did give me a lift. He regaled me with stories about his life which given his inebriated state was fairly incomprehensible. I kept on thinking, 'I need to get out of here', and was looking for an opportunity to excuse myself. He offered me a drink, I politely refused. His long suffering wife was trying to shut him up, but her efforts seemed to rev him up. When I felt there was a long pause in the one sided conversation I felt I could excuse myself and leave. As I walked out of the door I broke into a jog. I breathed a big sigh of relief. This short trip was actually the longest trip of the journey but I managed to get back to Auckland city centre and get the ferry back to Devonport and then home. Very tired but very relieved I had got back in one piece. My two friends had arrived at their respective homes many hours before me, but at least I had made it home safely.

Me and Don Hounsell on the hitch-hiking tour

Chapter Eighteen

DEVONPORT

O ur final move was back to Devonport. Walter and Dad had already gone back to the UK and not long after they left, Mum got us a house in Devonport. It was probably the best house we lived in. It was built on a hill overlooking Auckland Harbour and we could watch the ships coming in and out every day. The lights of Auckland harbour would be lit up; it was very beautiful. It was just two minutes to the beach and a fifteen minute walk to the shops of Devonport. We lived here for about a year and Giles and I finished our schooling and gained our School Certificates. Mum was working at the Naval Base in Devonport as a typist. She was very good at her job and received a commendation for her work.

I was enjoying New Zealand by this time. I was getting used to the culture, which was obviously different to Australia. New Zealand was more like Britain in many ways. A cooler climate than Australia, but not as cold as England. The North Island was much warmer than the South, the South is much more like the British climate. It was still a very much outdoors type of country with lots of activities centred around the beach and the sea and generally outdoor living. Like Australia, surfing, skiing and boating were popular activities. The population of New Zealand in the sixties was just over 2.5 million people. In contrast, the population of Great Britain at the time was 54.2 million people. The difference is staggering; New Zealand, geographically, is the size of Great Britain.

The Maoris, the indigenous people of New Zealand, are a lovely people and I got to know a few of them. We once went to Rotorua and saw a Maori settlement there. Rotorua was an amazing place with hot springs, bubbling mud, geysers and hot pools to swim or just lie in. There was a smell of sulphur in the air with all the geothermal activity going on.

We also had a boat ride through the glow worm caves. This was a starry wonderland of thousands of tiny creatures radiating a luminescent light in the subterranean world. It was an amazing experience. There

Bob, Walter and Giles at Glow Worm Caves in Waitomo

were many different levels, the tallest chamber in the cave was called 'The Cathedral'.

After finishing my school certificate (and in the summer holidays) I started earning money by advertising my services in the local paper. I put an ad in the local paper advertising my services as a decorator or willing to do any odd jobs. To my surprise, I got a call from someone who wanted me to paint their house. I thought of it as a challenge. I had done a bit of painting before but not on that scale. Fortunately, he showed me how to paint and what to do. The house was a very large wooden one as most houses were in those days. We agreed on $40, which was a ridiculously low amount even back then, but it was my first job and I was still learning. It took me just over a week to do the whole house. It was very tiring work, but I got it done. I was a bit annoyed I had priced myself so low, but I soon learnt how to paint. I am a bit of a perfectionist and I did a pretty good job of it if I say so myself. The owner of the house came round to see me from time to time and gave me good tips on how to achieve the best results. It led on to me getting another job with a painting firm and I found myself painting fishing boats.

This was a really interesting job. The person in charge had a business to paint fishing boats amongst other things. The decorators first of all sandblasted the metal boat getting rid of all the rust down to bare shiny metal while the boat was in dry dock. Then it was coated with red oxide paint. Next the boat was painted with an undercoat and a few coats of gloss paint. It took a while to paint these boats and I made pretty good money doing it. I did this for a few weeks during the summer holidays and thoroughly enjoyed it. It prepared me for future jobs when we got back to the UK.

I worked on my own once on a bank holiday. All the other decorators I was working with had time off but I was on my own painting this boat in Auckland Harbour. It was a smelly boat, the hold stank of rotten fish. I bought a hot pie and ate it for lunch. After a while painting in the hold I became so sick that I threw up. The boss came on the boat to check on me, and said he was impressed by my work. In many ways, I would have liked to continue working with them, they were a good team and I got on well with them. The decorating team also painted a metal bridge, which I was involved in helping with. Again, we sandblasted down to bare metal and then painted.

I got a small motor bike in my last year of New Zealand. It was a Lambretta scooter. A very nice bike which I bought for $25. It helped me get around and I went all over the place in it. It gave me a bit of credibility as I could have been mistaken for a mod. In those days you either had to be a mod, a rocker or a surfer. I was none of those really. I was once chatting with a group of people, boys and girls. One of the girls asked me 'Are you a mod, rocker or surfer?' 'I'm a surfer', I said, so as not to be embarrassed. She kept asking me questions and grilling me, which I found disconcerting. However, I thought I answered her questions fairly sensibly. Then she asked me what kind of surfboard I had and what 'stringer' the surfboard was. I had no idea what she meant. I mumbled 'well the board is my brother's actually'. She didn't ask any more questions after that. She knew, and I knew, she had caught me out. Naturally, I never saw her again.

My time at school ended because we were going to leave New Zealand and go back to England. My education was again interrupted which was a pity because I wanted to go into the sixth form and I think I would have done well.

I didn't feel cross about leaving New Zealand. I had really enjoyed my time there and made some really good friends but I was almost looking forward to going back to England. I was eighteen and could have stayed in New Zealand by myself. I thought about it. Where would I stay, what would I do? I could have gone into the sixth form for a couple of years (by the end of which I would have been twenty - this thought didn't appeal to me very much). I think I would have struggled on my own. I got to like New Zealand a lot. I still missed Australia though, for many different reasons. I was unsettled as to where my future lay. Australia, New Zealand or back in England.

I eventually made the decision to go back to England with Mum and Giles and rejoin Walter and Dad. It wasn't much of a choice really as I would have been on my own in New Zealand away from family, and I think family are the most important thing.

There was always this pull to go 'home' in my parents both when they lived in New Zealand and when we were in Australia. This was always unsettling for me. They of course wanted to see their relatives before they died, which was understandable. All our relatives were back in the UK and my Mum's mother was still alive and in her nineties. I think Mum could see if we had stayed in Australia or New Zealand we would have married and got settled down and we would never see our relatives again. It was a difficult decision for my parents because the lifestyle, weather and culture suited them very much. The pull for my parents to go back home was too strong.

Chapter Nineteen

LEAVING NEW ZEALAND

Leaving all our friends behind (once more) we set sail on the ship MS Shota Rustaveli. Peter Plummer and his wife came to see us off at the harbour. I thought it was very good of them. His parents had already gone back to the UK a year or two before. Peter and his family would follow later.

The MS Shota Rustaveli was a Russian ship with Russian crew. The crew were all very polite and courteous and spoke good English. It was a really enjoyable and interesting voyage. The ship sailed out of Auckland Harbour and past our house at North Head. We sailed through the harbour and up along the east coast of New Zealand. From there we had the long voyage to Tahiti which was the first stop. The whole trip to the UK would take several weeks.

We had a brilliant time on the ship. We got to eat well and relax as well. We watched movies, played games and socialised. We didn't actually see Mum much except at meal times and I think she enjoyed having some time to herself. Our cabins had bunk beds and I stayed in a cabin with three other older men. None of them really spoke to me much, so I didn't really get on with them. My brother Giles slept in another cabin. The cabins were very cramped, but they were only for sleeping in so we didn't mind too much. There was just one port hole to look out of. Needless to say I was seasick for the first few days, and I lay down on my bunk bed a lot during those days. After a few days I was okay and got my sea legs and felt alright.

I got lost once on the ship. I was exploring the ship and I found myself in the crew's quarters by accident. There was no one there fortunately, but on the walls were pictures of Stalin and Lenin. I thought I had better beat a hasty retreat and eventually found my way back.

During our meal times in the restaurant we were served by Russian waiters and waitresses: they were very polite. The food was excellent and one time we had caviar. Across from where we were sitting sat a young couple probably in their mid to late thirties. A young lad was sitting with them who would have been about seventeen. He had long, blond hair. We didn't speak to them much but they seemed to be a nice family. We were allocated the same table every day. We usually said a greeting to them when they arrived and sat down. Every day they would eat at the same table and they would be chatting away to each other. We only ever saw them at meal times. We didn't know at the time the young lad was a stowaway. He had boarded in New Zealand. Apparently, he had spotted a married couple who looked a bit like him and decided to join them at the meal table. I don't know where he slept, but probably on deck. What gave him away was there was a pyjama party one night for the young people. Photos were being taken and his photo was taken. The eagle-eyed captain of the ship realised there was something wrong and he wasn't supposed to be travelling on board. How he knew it from the photo I don't know, but he must have done some investigating. When we docked at Tahiti he was promptly taken off the ship and put on a flight back to where he came from. It was all very exciting. We only knew the story when the couple next came in for lunch without the young lad. We asked where their 'son' was and they told us all the news.

On board there was a Russian shop which sold lots of Russian souvenirs. Mum bought me a Russian fur hat which cost a lot of money. I asked the Russian lady assistant if she could exchange some English money for Roubles. 'Nyet, nyet' she shouted and waved her hands. A few minutes later I found myself alone on one of the decks staring out to sea. A Russian crew member came up behind me and tapped me on the shoulder and rather furtively said, "You want Rouble?" He looked cautiously around him to make sure no-one was looking. I thought it was a bit strange that he thought he might have got into trouble by exchanging a rouble with me. I gave him a New Zealand dollar which was the exchange rate at the time. He went away very happy. I hoped it was the correct rate and I hoped he was going to be alright and not get into any trouble.

One day, early on in the voyage, I was with Giles sunbathing and had fallen asleep. Giles left me on deck and went off somewhere and left me alone sleeping. I woke up some time later and felt very sore. I don't know how long I was asleep for. The whole of my chest was red raw and I knew I was seriously sunburnt. We were not far from Tahiti at the time, so it was really hot. I went to the medical station and they gave me some cream to put on. However my chest came out in blisters and it would take a while for it to heal. It was very painful. It was also very annoying as we were only a week or so into our journey. We had about three or four more weeks to go, and I was in agony.

Tahiti was a beautiful island full of beautiful people. The ship docked in Papeete and we were able to get off and spend the day there. It was very hot and there was a dance arranged with some of the beautiful young women in their Tahitian costumes. When I say costumes I mean grass skirts. Much as I wanted to, I couldn't dance with these beautiful girls as I was so sore from the blisters. Ah well, never mind. We had a drink and lunch on the island and enjoyed exploring. I can see why the famous painter Gauguin wanted to live there. It was utterly idyllic with its sunshine, beautiful white sandy beaches, clear blue water and relaxed lifestyle.

The next leg of our journey took several days and we were heading for the Panama Canal. A very narrow canal, which had to be taken very slowly. We stopped a few times and it was interesting to see the people on both sides of America. One one side of the canal they were in North America and South America on the other. We finally got through and we turned right out of the canal and stopped off at Curaçao. This was a wonderful island and again very hot. We stopped for a day here and Giles and I explored the island. We couldn't do much in a day. I would have looked forward to going swimming from one of the beautiful beaches but we didn't have time. I'm not sure what Mum did, I think she went off somewhere to explore as well, but we met up again for a coffee and lunch. The islanders were pleased to see us and we were sorry to leave. The last bit of the journey would not take long, just a few days across the Atlantic Ocean and we would be back in England. This was probably the worst bit of the journey. There was nothing to see for days and days. Just the rough Atlantic Ocean. I noticed after a while the temperature was getting very, very cold; colder by the day. From about 30 degrees in Curaçao to about -5 degrees as we headed towards England. I had not known cold for a long time.

So began another journey as we arrived in England.

Chapter Twenty

BACK IN ENGLAND

We arrived in Southampton in March 1971 and when we docked it was freezing cold and snowing. We had not seen snow for 10 years, so it was a bit of a novelty for us boys. But we sure weren't ready for the icy, cold weather. We were used to very hot temperatures in Australia and New Zealand and to come back to this was awful. I thought to myself, 'What have we come back to?' It was all new to me, coming back to England. I hardly knew what England was like. I was going to find out soon enough. We were not suitably dressed for such cold weather. No coats and no warm clothes.

As I mentioned, Walter and Dad went back to the UK a year before Giles, Mum and me. So they stayed in New Zealand for only four years. They went back to the UK by ship on the 5th Feb 1970. Walter was eighteen at the time. The ship was called the 'SS Akaroa'.

The idea was for Dad and Walter to find a place to live and Dad to get some a job to prepare the way for the rest of us when we left New Zealand and arrived back in the UK a year later. We didn't hear from either Dad or Walter when they got back to UK so we presumed everything was okay. Later, we found out they stayed with Dad's friends and then at

Aunt Kate's for a while. Then they stayed in London before renting a flat in Oxford. At one point in their stay in the UK, Dad decided to fly back to New Zealand. I think he must have had some sort of aberration. This was not in the plan! He caught a plane with money given by Aunt Kate. The plane stopped off in Spain and at this point Dad must have decided against the trip, staying in Spain for a few days before flying back to the UK. I don't know what he was thinking.

He left poor old Walter on his own for a while. Walter at the time couldn't really manage without the financial assistance from Dad and would probably have ended up on the streets. When Dad did get back to the UK he really struggled financially. To make ends meet, Dad sold practically everything he had. On top of this, when Dad was away for a few days in Spain Walter lost his job as a radio technician. So Walter and Dad had a difficult time during the year, moving from place to place, staying with friends or relatives houses for a time and hostels, boarding houses and flats. Dad was too old to work by now and Walter not settled in any job. Dad went by bus with a suitcase full of first edition books which he hoped to sell in Central London. He stowed the suitcase in the luggage rack. When he got off at his stop the suitcase had gone. Someone had stolen it. Probably hundreds of pounds worth of books just gone! A very expensive bus ride!

Eventually, we heard from them and our arrangements were made. We were met by Walter and Dad at Southampton docks. Unfortunately, no one else came to see us at the docks. What I didn't know as Dad greeted us was, he not only didn't have a job but he didn't have a house or any type of accommodation for us to live in. He had given up his rented property in Oxford and hadn't arranged anywhere for us to stay. We were faced with the prospect of nowhere to live. Well it took some explaining! There was some miscommunication between Dad and Mum about who was going to greet us at the docks. Mum was expecting her sisters to be there and some other relatives, but somehow they never got the message and so no one greeted us except Dad and Walter. This wasn't a good start to our arrival in the UK. Needless to say Mum was more than a little upset.

We caught a train to London not knowing where we were eventually going to live. As we journeyed on the train coming in to London, what hit me most was all the houses seemed the same and they all seemed so cramped together. It was so different from New Zealand and Australia (especially) with its vast openness. As the song goes, *Little boxes all made of ticky-tacky*. I was quickly getting depressed. Then there were the high rise tenement blocks! Surely people can't live in those I thought to myself. I had not seen those before. We arrived at Waterloo station with our bags. We waited a long time in London basically because we had nowhere to stay. Walter was used to being in London by this time and wanted to show me and Giles the underground among other things which I thought was brilliant. I had never seen anything like it and the fact we could travel for miles underneath the city: it was fantastic. We forgot our troubles for a time. While we boys were out enjoying ourselves on the London underground Mum was busy making arrangements to find somewhere for us all to stay that night and for a few nights afterwards. I don't think Dad could see what the problem was. Mum must have found somewhere because we were on the move again. We were going to stay in this horrible hostel in Maidstone in the freezing cold weather in March. We were not used to such cold weather and it was pretty miserable. We spent the time having snowball fights and looking around the town. There was not much else to do. The hostel was terrible, with no adequate heating. I'm sure it was frequented by ex-prisoners from the local jail. The room I was in was dire. For a headboard it had a piece of vinyl stuck to the wall by the bed. For heating, you had to put some money in the coin slot and the heating would come on but only for a few minutes just enough time to get into bed before it ran out. Welcome to England! I was sitting around the TV just wanting to relax in the lounge, but there were six or so men in there, all staring vacantly at the TV. There was something boring on the screen and I said, 'Does anyone mind if I turn it over?' No response from anyone. So I turned over to a different channel. Again there was no response. They just stared blankly at the TV. I thought it was just a bit creepy.

As I mentioned previously, my parents didn't communicate with us kids much about anything, so we were never really sure what was happening or where we were going to live. After a couple of weeks they had found a house to live in a place called Enstone in Oxfordshire. It is where we headed to and were to live at least for the next three or four years. It wasn't a bad place really. It was a two bedroom annex attached to a much larger four bedroom house in the middle of the village. The owner of the house was an ex-Squadron Leader and his wife. A lovely couple who made us feel welcome and didn't mind our disparate family.

There were just two bedrooms for the five of us. This meant at least one of us boys, usually Giles or me, had to sleep on a put you up mattress in the living room and then tidy it up the next day. We all then had to quickly find jobs. Mum was quite quick in getting a job and she found one with the Ministry of Agriculture, Fisheries and Food as a clerk typist in Oxford. It was otherwise known as the 'Min of Ag and Fish' for short. It was two bus rides for her, to Oxford and then out to the outskirts. The long bus ride to Oxford which took about forty minutes. It was a long day for her, she got back from work about 6.30pm and then had to cook tea as Dad didn't really do much at all when he was at home. Dad would have

Mum and Dad

been 67, but looked more like 77. He couldn't get a job at his age even if he tried, but he didn't try. He rather enjoyed not having to go to work.

We didn't have a car for a while, but Walter bought an old Mini Van. It was a wreck of a car, and we spent most of our time pop riveting the body work because bits kept falling off. There was even a hole in the floor boards. For the first year or two, I went around barefoot and even hitch-hiked to London, once, barefoot. I didn't think anything of it, after all we went barefoot all the time in Australia and a lot of the time in New Zealand. Walter even went for a job interview barefoot! We soon realised perhaps it wasn't the best thing to do and so our acquired Australian customs gradually diminished. As well as our accents. I had a strong Aussie accent which gradually diminished in New Zealand and then coming back to England I seemed to lose it altogether. I now have a fairly neutral accent.

I used to do a lot of hitch-hiking in those days. I didn't have a car and I usually couldn't afford the bus or train fare. I would often hitch-hike to various cities like London, Birmingham and Oxford. I liked looking around the cities and do a lot of window shopping. I would spend the day, have lunch and hitch-hike home. One time after I had hitch-hiked to London I wanted to hitch hike back to Oxford. I started hitch hiking back home in the late afternoon. Unfortunately, for me I was hitch-hiking on the wrong road out of London. I was on the M1 when I should have been on the M40. As I was waiting to get a lift, another guy was also hitch-hiking, came up to me and said, 'I've got a knife and I want all your money'. All I had was a pound, so I gave it to him. He muttered something and wasn't very happy but soon disappeared, thankfully. I finally got a lift, to Leicester. The driver had stopped off at a service station for some reason and then was heading back to London. (I wondered if there was a dodgy deal going on). He dropped me off in the middle of nowhere and pointed to a road which would take me towards Oxford. I finally got into work after nine hours of hitch-hiking and walking, at exactly the time I was supposed to have started 6am the next day! I was tired and exhausted.

Walter (20) and Bob (18) on holiday

When we arrived in 1971 we saw adverts on the TV inviting people to go out to Australia for ten pounds. The adverts weren't shown for long though as the scheme ended in 1972. I remember them saying English people always played croquet on the lawn with the vicar drinking tea and jam scones. The advert literally showed English people playing croquet with a vicar. I think the idea was you could have a better life than this down under. Ironically, we did have a croquet set which we played with quite a bit in Australia and New Zealand (it even travelled back with us in our boxes).

We encountered decimalisation, yet again. The new currency didn't phase me this time as I had got well and truly used to the decimal system and much preferred it to the old system of pounds, shillings and pence. Not sure how my parents coped with it though.

We boys all tried to look for work. Giles worked on a building site for a while. Walter found work in a local hospital in Oxford. I tried looking for work in Oxford. I went to the local Employment Exchange as it was known then to register with them and to get help with finding work. I was able to get a small amount of unemployment benefit from them, but not really enough to live on. My big stumbling block was lack of qualifications. It seemed no employer would recognise my New Zealand School Certificate. So I had to write to New Zealand House to verify that New Zealand School Certificate was equivalent to UK GCE's, which they did, eventually. It seemed particularly difficult to get work in Oxford in the early 1970s. I remember overhearing a conversation one man had at the Exchange saying to one of the Clerks, 'But I've got an HND in Business Studies'. It didn't seem to matter, there was no work.

A lady from the Employment Exchange came to our house in Enstone. She wanted to see me about work. I think it was about eight in the morning and I was still on the camp bed in the living room. Dad said to her, 'Oh, do come in', knowing full well I was still in bed. So she came into the living room where I was sleeping and I had to scramble out of bed half naked, get some clothes on in another room and then come back and speak to her about work. She harangued me about the fact I should have been up much earlier looking for work. I said to her I didn't think it would make any difference if I looked for work at seven am or looked for work at nine am. It was not as if I didn't try. I certainly tried to find work but it was difficult.

Willing to do anything, I took a job at Fortes Motel in Oxford. Most people who applied could get work because the pay was so poor. I was paid 17 ½ pence per hour. Even in those days it was bad. My job was to pour tea and coffee all day. There was a queue of people, often several hundred, every day. It was relentless. Every day, coachloads of people would arrive in the car park. It cost me 35p on the bus to get there for the single journey which took a chunk of my day's wages. So I hitch-hiked to work every morning at six for months. I got a lift with all sorts of interesting people. Once I got a lift in a chauffeur driven Rolls Royce.

The driver kindly dropped me off right outside work and I'm sure my colleagues were looking on as I got out of the car. In the end, I got so fed up with working for almost nothing I decided to go back to college and try and get some more qualifications.

When I enrolled at Banbury Technical College, I had the chance of doing a course in the Art school. I had a look around. But the students I saw in the Art Department looked bored and didn't seem to be doing anything much. Later, I had an interview with the Careers Advisor who asked me what I wanted to do. I said 'Art'. She told me 'There is an Art School here in the College'. I said 'Yes, I know. But I don't want to go to that Art School'. She pulled a face and said, 'So, you want to do Art but you don't want to go to college. Well I can't help you then'. She closed her book and got up to go. This was the end of the conversation which took all of three minutes; and I walked out. 'Thanks for nothing', I thought to myself. If she had probed a bit more deeply and asked me why I didn't want to go I would have said I had slight misgivings about the course. This could have easily been discussed and surmounted, but was rather cut short by an inept Careers Guidance Counsellor who wasn't prepared to listen.

While I was at Banbury College, I was wandering down town and happened to go into Woolworths looking for something. An elderly man came up to me quite randomly and said 'I believe you are looking for a Church'. As it happened I was. He didn't know it, but having just arrived from New Zealand I hadn't found a Church to go to and desperately wanted to find one. I of course replied, 'Yes, I am.' He looked a bit taken aback. The next Sunday I went to his Church, which was the Banbury Baptist Church. I was made to feel really welcome. They met in the Town Hall. The old man who invited me was called Eddie Plank, a music teacher. He invited me to lunch during the week when I was at College and I used to go to his house quite regularly for a nice hot meal. He and his wife were lovely people and I will never forget their love and generosity.

164

However, going to college didn't really help my education. I didn't do so well, and only gained one GCE O level. So in the same year, 1972, I decided to join the Royal Air Force (RAF). I went to the Careers Information office in Oxford and one thing led to another. I had to do several tests which I presumably passed, much to my surprise as my confidence levels were at rock bottom. I think I might have surprised the Carcers Information Officer (CIO).

While I waited to go into the RAF I got a part time job as a postman in the village. I was working two shifts, two or three hours in the morning and then later in the afternoon for a couple of hours. It was brilliant. I loved the job and might have been a postman as a career move except I was waiting to go in the RAF. I worked with an older lady who took me under her wing. She was really lovely and helped me a lot as I was trying to deliver letters to the right addresses. I made a few mistakes but my new-found friend was really supportive and helpful. I had to get up at 5am every day: an early start but it got me into the discipline of work which was really helpful. I realised you can't get anywhere in life if you don't work hard. I got to know all the people in the village and I was mostly greeted with a smile by my customers as everyone likes to receive letters in the post. I was working right up to the time I was to join the Royal Air Force.

I decided I wanted to be in the RAF Police and after a bit of waiting I found myself posted to a place called RAF Swinderby in November 1972. Dad came with me to London to see me off. He bought me lunch and a knickerbocker glory, a very nice treat. I didn't know what I was letting myself in for. I got the train which took me to Lincoln and then a bus to RAF Swinderby. My real education began when I joined the RAF and I did numerous qualifications during my 22 years stint. In the end, I didn't join the police, but was offered a job as an RAF Telegraphist. That's another story.

Giles by then had done an Art course in Oxford gaining an A level. He worked for a time in a paint shop called 'Manders' in Oxford. This had

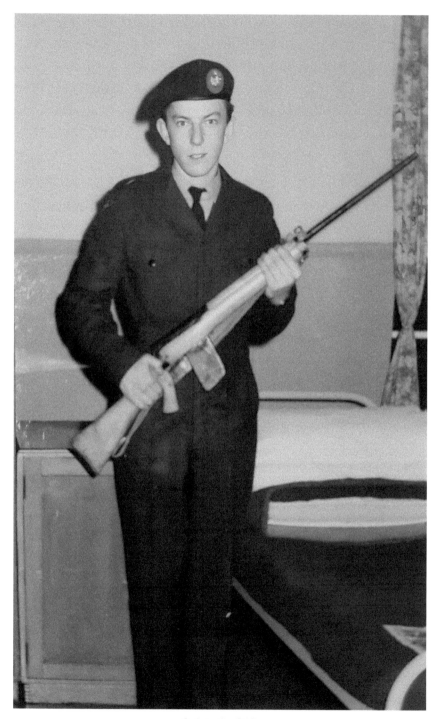

Bob in the RAF

special significance because my father knew a lady called Rosalie Mander who had been a student at Oxford University with him and he was very fond of her. Much later she came to our house in Enstone and showed us a book which she had written and published. It was said in the family my Father had wanted to marry Rosalie. But instead, she married Geoffrey Mander whose family owned the Mander group, a principal employer selling paints, inks and varnishes throughout the UK.

Giles left this job and rather bravely gave up work and studied Drama at an acting school in London for three years. Years later, he completed an Art Degree at Central St Martin's. He also went to a mime School in France for a year. He met, and later married Tamsin at the acting school who also became an actor. Giles graduated from the acting college and became an actor doing very well. They had three children two girls and a boy. Giles appeared in many adverts and also appeared in theatre and the movie *Shadowlands* and also as a butler in an Agatha Christie movie. Their children, Oscar, Vita and Daisy have all done very well for themselves and live in Oxford. Sadly, Giles was diagnosed with Parkinsons in early 2000 and died in 2021. He bravely fought it for many years and was always good humoured and never complained.

Walter did very well in the end, after a few rocky starts in his working life. He was a confirmed bachelor for most of his life. He became a self-employed gardener as a young man in his twenties. Walter found his true vocation in life (working for an employer in full time employment didn't really suit him). He loved gardening and became quite an expert. After a few years he did very well for himself and always had work. He had a number of clients and was always busy, sometimes too busy. He would often work six days a week. He became a Christian not long after he came to the UK and after I arrived.

Walter and I used to do more things together after he became a Christian. Life changed for him and he started going to Church. Like me, he loved going to Church, reading the Bible and praying. He had found a peace and a joy which he never really had before. My younger brother Giles never pursued it, although he did have a profession of faith at Arapohue Camp. He never followed it up for some reason. We brothers were very close and we all tried to get on with each other and despite our differences we got on very well.

I was really pleased Walter was going to the same Church I was going to. Becoming a Christian really changed him and one of the first things he did was go to a Bible College for a year to get grounding in Christian teaching. After his year at College he was engaged in a lot of missionary work (entirely voluntarily) alongside his normal paid work. One of his mission trips was to spend a year in Russia helping and supporting street children through a Christian Charity. He didn't get paid, he had to fund himself for a year which I thought was incredible. He also went to Uganda many times helping out with missionaries he got to know. He learnt to pilot an aircraft and flew from Banbury to Lincolnshire to see me one time. He married late in life, when he was 64 to a lovely Philipino lady called Gen. They still live happily in Banbury.

Chapter Twenty-One

ANY REGRETS?

Do I have any regrets going to Australia or New Zealand? No, not at all. Je ne regrette rien. It was a great education. Although my formal education didn't amount to much, going to Australia really broadened my horizons. It allowed me to see and absorb a very different culture. Going to another country and experiencing the culture seems to clear your mind of a whole load of junk. I believe you can see life from a different perspective. You can become more tolerant and accepting of people. I believe in the value of experiencing life in other countries. It may mean more than just going on holiday for a couple of weeks and seeing the tourist sites. It means taking in the culture and seeing how people live and work. For all my problems and difficulties integrating with the Australian culture and the racism I experienced especially in Australia I am very grateful for the rich experience of living with people of other cultures and languages. Yes, I did find it difficult adjusting to life in the different countries and places. It was heart wrenching at times and very challenging to suddenly find yourself in another country and we experienced it three times.

It is said you need to be in a place for forty years before you are really accepted. As we were only ever in one place for a short length of time,

I never felt accepted or had any sense of belonging. I tried hard to fit in to the different cultures, but it was difficult as we always seemed to be travelling through. I found myself constantly having to adjust.

However, the positive experience outweighed the negative. The experience has been helpful in my becoming less discriminatory of other people. I found once you integrate yourself with the local people they quickly become friendly and helpful. I learned about segregation and discrimination for the first time and how the Aboriginals were treated at the time. I learnt about adapting to the culture of the country, and assimilating into their way of life. I believe living in other countries broadens one's perspective on life. It makes one see there is something else in life. It has made me more resourceful and less dependent on others for well-being. It has made me a happier person and more rounded person. I have become more broadminded as a person.

I think I can now identify with people who feel discriminated against in our society, vulnerable people, women, people of different ethnic or cultural backgrounds, people of colour, because I've experienced some of these prejudices, even as a white person.

I know people who have never lived outside their little village and never even been to the local town or city. I think it is very sad. To not even have experienced life outside their own little world. I wouldn't want to be parochial and isolationist.

If I hadn't gone to Australia and New Zealand things would have been very different for me in England. I might well have been still living in a council house going out with my mates. I could have easily fallen in with the wrong crowd and who knows what might have happened. We can't live life with an 'if only' attitude. I don't look at the past with regret or what might have been. It is just a waste of time as far as I'm concerned. Life is too short for regrets or looking back. I can say we really made a go of it in Australia and New Zealand. I'm glad we didn't come back sooner like so many others did. We were not going to be 'Boomerang Poms'.

As it was, I made friends, some of whom I have contact with to this day. I certainly wouldn't have the breadth of experience I have today. No formal education can give you it. The whole experience has helped me push myself out of my comfort zone and has really stretched me.

Living in poverty in Australia taught me you don't always need a lot of money to be happy. We certainly didn't have a lot of money, but we enjoyed life. The experience has also helped me to work hard making sure my family were provided for and we could look after ourselves. Being poor during my childhood years was a good thing for me. It helped to spur me on to buy a house of my own. My parents never owned a house in their lives. They could have done, they had plenty of opportunity. In Australia, land and houses were so cheap. But my parents were not savvy with money. They seemed to have a loose affiliation with it, and they were always struggling financially. I was determined not to be in the same position.

This could have been difficult because I think children tend to copy or emulate their parents' lifestyle. This is not always true and certainly not for me. I bought my first house when I was 28. I was the first in my family to own a house, albeit a small two bedroom terraced house for £4,000. This was cheap even in 1979 when I bought it. I worked hard and made sure I was never out of a job. Although I was not a high earner, I wanted a steady job to support wife and family.

How I Met My Wife

Wendy had been working in London and decided that she wanted a break and chose to go to Sleaford in Lincolnshire, partly because of cheap housing. She applied for a job at Interflora Headquarters who were advertising for a male marketing administrator. She said to the head of HR would they consider a woman. They looked at her references and she got the job. Later, after a divorce, she started going to the Church I was attending. She was seeking something more out of life. I must admit I looked at this pretty woman and thought 'Wow, I wouldn't mind going out with her'. I had bought a small house in Sleaford and was house sharing with a few male friends of mine. One of my friends, Richard, was friendly with Wendy and told me that Wendy really liked me. Our Church had a Church weekend away with a whole group of us going. As we were in a small group I started noticing Wendy and she noticed me. A few weeks later I summoned up the courage to ask her out for a date. We went to the local Chinese restaurant for our first date and got to

Wendy and I on our Wedding Day

know each other over the coming weeks. This was October/ November 1980. We started seeing each other quite a bit. Then one day I said to her, 'Wendy, will you marry me?' That took all my courage. To my amazement she said 'Yes'. Things moved fairly fast after that. I took her to see my parents in Oxford. (My Dad once said to Mum, 'Bobby will come home one day and say he is going to get married' –and that's what I did). We got married on the 7th February 1981 in Sleaford. It was a lovely mild sunny day and there were about 80 guests present. After the service we had a wedding reception and then Wendy and I caught the train to London for our honeymoon where we spent a few days. We had booked first class and when we came back on the train there were no seats available and we had to sit in the guards van sitting on a barrel. But we didn't mind – we were in love. We have been married now for 42 years. Not long after we got married a friend said to Wendy 'How's married life?' Wendy replied, 'It's great, Bob and I have so much fun together'. The friend looked shocked as if to say 'you can't have fun if you're married'. But we have good fun, we enjoy each other's company and love each other.

Wendy and I at our Wedding Breakfast

Our Children

Daniel our first born is married to Jess and they have two lovely daughters, Harriet and Lucy, six and three at the time of writing. Daniel works for a major motorcycle company as Strategic Planner and Jess works in HR for Oxford University

Jonathan our second son, lives in New York and works as a Researcher for a major company that helps businesses run more effectively. He has just recently got married to Victoria and we went to their wedding ceremony and reception in Italy this year. It was a wonderful occasion with over a hundred guests. Victoria works for Microsoft heading up the Teams development team.

Miriam our youngest works as a nurse, graduating from Oxford Brookes and now lives in Liverpool and is working as a TB nurse. She is married to Rob and they have a lovely son, Albie, who is two years old.

Brothers Return

My brothers and I went back to Australia in 2012 for a three week holiday. Giles, flew out first and went to New Zealand. Walter and I flew out to Brisbane a week later. Walter and I arrived in Brisbane and met up with Giles at the airport. We stayed at an airport hotel for a night. The next day, we got a taxi and went around Brisbane to see where we lived and went to school. We saw our school, the East Brisbane State School. It seemed tiny. As there was no one there we had a quick look round. It certainly bought back some memories. When we were kids it seemed huge.

Brisbane had certainly changed a lot since last we went in the sixties. It is now a very modern and vibrant city with plenty of restaurants, eateries and big department stores. We stayed in a hotel in the city centre for the night and the following day we were going to see where we lived for five years. We arrived by train to Cleveland late morning and stayed in a B&B for a couple of days, with a lovely couple just on the outskirts. We soon travelled to Victoria Point to have a look around. One of the first things we did was to take a ferry ride to Coochiemudlo. What had changed in all those years? Well the jetty had changed. A brand new one. But the island seemed pretty much the same except there were no mud pools. It was all sandy beaches. Exploring the island we saw beautiful well maintained bungalows. There was just the one shop on the island. A local resident met with us and we chatted for a while. He had emigrated from Canada and loved living on the island. I thought 'What a great place to live! Your own desert island.'

We got on the ferry back to the mainland and looked at the few shops at the Point and saw what was probably our first house which seemed the same. We then walked the coastal path to O'Halloran Point. In the sixties there was no such path, just the beach and mud flats. We didn't recognize the place, it was so different. There were houses everywhere. O'Halloran Point had become a quality tourist destination and a place of historical and cultural interest in a conservation area. On the site we lived on there must have been dozens of houses; some with swimming pools. Swimming pools?! All we had back then was a leaky tin canoe.

Walter, me and Giles outside our old school

A lot of the houses were overlooking the ocean. There was also a shopping mall in Victoria Point, on the outskirts. All the shops you need with cafés and restaurants. Much had changed in Australia as expected. We got on really well with everyone, and people were very friendly and helpful. We stayed in Cleveland for a couple of days. We visited our old school, Victoria Point State School. From the outside it looked much the same. We didn't go in as the children were in school and we didn't want to disturb them. The children all had smart school uniforms and were wearing hats. In the sixties, we didn't have school uniforms and were not told of the dangers of the sun, so didn't bother with hats or sun cream. It bought back many memories.

We left Cleveland and Victoria Point and continued our adventures up north. We travelled from Brisbane to Noosa by train and stayed a few days with a delightful couple. They looked after us very well, providing meals

Walter, Giles and I outside our old school

and giving us a guided tour around Noosa. We then left and headed for Fraser Island.

Fraser Island Antics

On Fraser Island we were escorted around the island by a tour guide in a large 10 seater 4x4. He was a young guy in his 30s. He enjoyed talking a lot and during the course of the trip he said he had a $100 challenge. He would give $100 to anyone who can bend right down on one leg while lifting the other leg straight out'. He then proceeded to demonstrate. No one took him up on the challenge during the course of the next few days. However on the last day when Giles, Walter and I were being dropped off to catch the ferry back to the mainland Giles said to the tour guide, 'I want to take you up on your challenge'. Giles then proceeded to complete the challenge. The tour guide's mouth dropped open. For once he was speechless. I said to him, 'Not bad for someone who's got Parkinsons'. I think you owe us a $100'. He never did pay us.

In the back of the Fraser Island Transport

Next we headed for Cairns were we stayed for a few days in a back packers hostel which was surprisingly very good. We had a tour of the Great Barrier Reef and had a swim and saw all the beautiful fish and colourful coral.

We also spent one day travelling to the world heritage rainforest using the cable car, going up to Kuranda village. The trip up was incredible, passing just over the rainforest canopy. The village itself was amazing with lots of art and craft shops and a wildlife centre. At the end of the day we caught the train down and viewed the incredible scenery. We got a coach going back to Cairns and on the way the driver said, 'In a minute you are going to see something really amazing. Look out to the right, look, there, there', pointing to a house, 'That house is over a hundred years old.' I thought it was rather amusing considering the ages of some of our houses back in the UK. Afterwards, we took a plane to Darwin.

Walter and Giles stayed in Darwin for a week, but I had to get back to UK. We had a great time. The people were really friendly and helpful.

I'd like to go back to Australia and New Zealand again sometime.

I am eternally grateful for the decision my parents made when they flicked a coin and said 'It's heads. We are going to Australia'.

ADDITIONAL PHOTOS

There are a number of photos from my story which I want to include as they help 'set-the-scene' of my experience which didn't quite fit into the narrative, so I have included them in this appendix.

The Drawing Room at Fernley

One of the many study rooms at Fernley

The Dining Room at Fernley

Fernley Croquet Lawn

Exterior View of Fernley

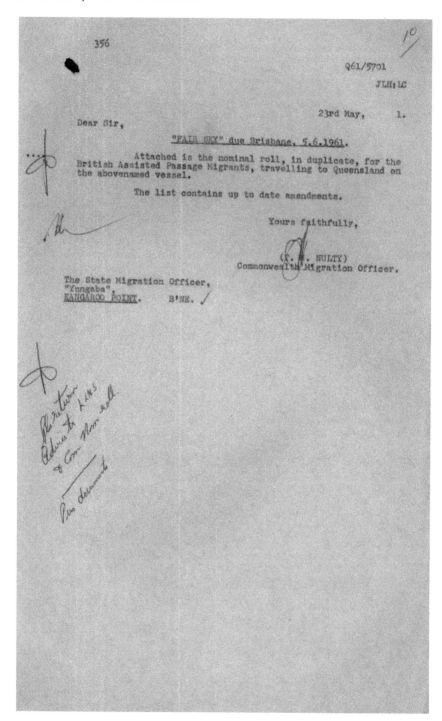

356

Q61/5701

JLH:LC

23rd May,   1.

Dear Sir,

"FAIR SKY" due Brisbane, 5.6.1961.

Attached is the nominal roll, in duplicate, for the British Assisted Passage Migrants, travelling to Queensland on the abovenamed vessel.

The list contains up to date amendments.

Yours faithfully,

(T. J. NULTY)
Commonwealth Migration Officer.

The State Migration Officer,
"Yungaba",
KANGAROO POINT.   B'NE.

Front section of Yungaba Manifest from the Fairsky

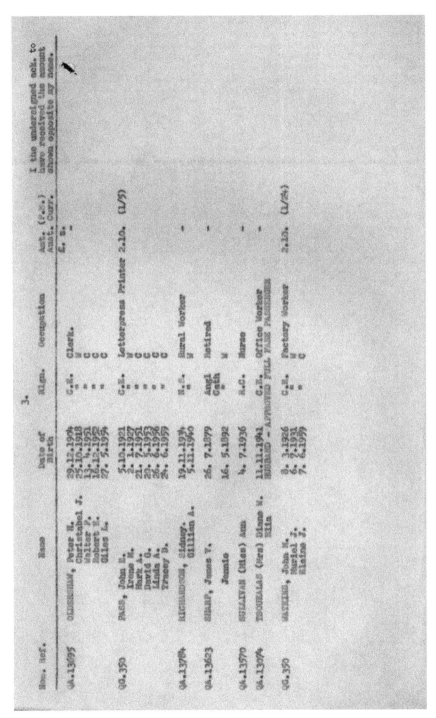

Page 3 of Yungaba Manifest from the Fairsky

Me at a Maori settlement about age 15

Walter aged 30.

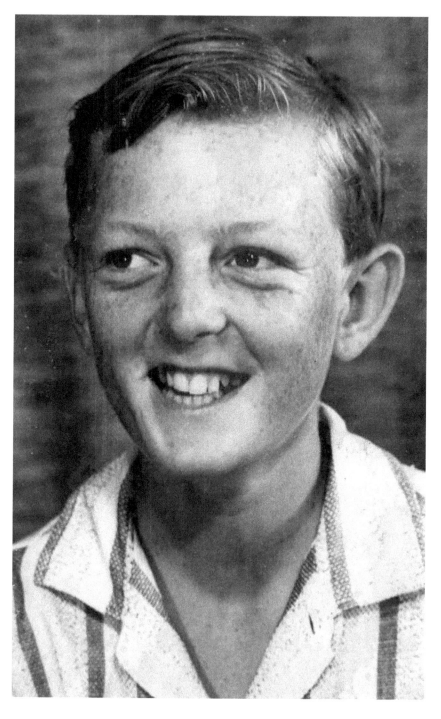

Giles about age 13

Walter Back Row, 4th from the Left. Me Back Row, 4th from Right.

Phoning Wendy for a Date

ADDITIONAL INFORMATION ON ALL THE PHOTOS

All of the photos have captions but in some instances I wanted to explain in more detail to provide you with further context and also credit the source where necessary.

Chapter 1

Page 4

We spent a lot of time relaxing on the deck. Here Dad is on the left, Giles in the middle and Mum on the right.

Page 5

In one of the bars, Dad, Walter and Mum with one of Dad's friends, Charlie (who later came to see us at Halloran Point).

Page 7

The Nominal Role of Asssisted Passage Migrants (pg. 7), Listed my Surname and then forename and initals. Taken from the National Archives of Australia (J25, 1961/5701).

Page 8

The Fairsky at sea. Photo credit to Torrens. Taken from Ship Nostagia website.

Chapter 2

Page 12

Mum and Dad in London, about 1949 soon after they married.

Page 15

Fernley Manor, from the croquet lawn.

Page 16

Family photo – me on the left talking to Aunt Woozle with Mum and Dad. Walter on Dad's shoulder and Giles on his knee. Dad looking very old, but actually only about 54.

Page 18

A rare photo of my Father sitting with the famous author G K Chesterton. Dad was a regular visitor and became like a son to GKC. This photo was featured in the National Portrait Gallery.

Page 21

Mum's family. From left, her sisters Greta and Pam, her mother, Nora, and my Mum on right.

Chapter 3

Page 27

Me by the River Thames, with our beloved dog Sappho.

Chapter 4

Page 35

On board ship all at sea. I am on the left, with Giles.

Page 36

I am on the right with Giles, We were ready to play a game of bowls on deck.

Page 38

A certificate given to everyone when the ship crossed the equator. The date 18th May 1961.

Chapter 6

Page 44

A typical transit hut where migrants would be housed – for days, weeks or months. Very basic as it wasn't intended for long stays.

Page 45

Yungaba Immigration Centre Main Building.

Page 46

A note from the Fairsky Manifest stating our luggage was to follow on the FairSea.

Chapter 7

Page 53 (1)

Relaxing on the beach at Coochiemudlo. Norma Bishop on left. Mum with no hat on and another two ladies whose names are unknown.

Page 53 (2)

Mum on the far right, scratching her eye. Norma Bishop is seated. They are with their group of farm workers having a 'smoko' break.

Page 55

Our lovely Mum, sat on the rocks at Coochiemudlo.

Chapter 8

Page 60

This is an iconic photo, possibly taken by Charlie, Dad's friend from the ship. At our house in Halloran Point. Giles on left, Walter and me on right with Dad and Mum. I'm wondering what was going on in Mum's mind.

Page 63

Dad at Halloran Point. Skinny as a rake, he nearly always went shirtless.

Page 65

On the beach with Dad, me on the left Giles and Walter.

Chapter 9

Page 72

A copy of our school register at Victoria Point State School.

Page 74

Victoria Point State School Register of Corporal Punishment. I couldn't find an entry with my name. Maybe they only kept a sample of the records...

Page 81

On the jetty at Victoria Point. We had just received these toy guns as a Christmas present. Two weeks later they were stolen. Giles on left, Walter in the centre and me on the right.

Page 84

Me walking up from the beach at O'Halloran Point. It was near this spot that dad threw a lighted match on the ground and set fire to 36 acres.

Chapter 12

Page 95

Taken at our next house in Link Road. Giles on left, Walter (seated) me on right and Dad. In the tin shack at the back lived three generations of the Coolwell family who became friends of ours.

Page 96

The Coolwell family. The girl on the left is Gwen and the girl on the right Elsie (of whom I was fond).

Page 97

Mum, still looking very wistful. Preparing a meal on a wood stove at our Link Road house.

Page 98

Mum, proudly showing off our utility vehicle. We boys would sit in the back when we went anywhere.

Page 101

Me seated on left, with Giles, Mum and Walter. A year later we would be moving to New Zealand.

Page 104

Cleveland yacht club, where I learned how to sail.

Chapter 13

Page 111

Walter and Giles larking about at Devonport Harbour. I am on the right.

Page 112

Giles, Walter and I at Rotorua.

Page 115

Mum starting on the front steps at our first house in Devonport.

Chapter 14

Page 121

Me, Walter and Giles as part of the St. John Ambulance Brigade. Looking smart in our uniforms.

Chapter 16

Page 132

At Arapohue Bush Camp, New Zealand. I was a youth leader of a group of boys. I am second from left at back.

Page 133

Me standing outside one of the tin huts I helped to build.

Chapter 17

Page 140

A view of a North Island town we passed through 'on tour'.

Page 142

Don Hounsell and John Harrop the two friends with whom I hitch-hiked around New Zealand.

Page 145

Me and Don Hounsell on our hitch-hiking tour.

Chapter 18

Page 148

Me, Walter and Giles at the Glow Worm caves in Waitomo on a day out.

Chapter 20

Page 160

Mum and Dad at Quarry Cottage, Enstone, Oxfordshire.

Page 162

Walter and me on holiday when we were 20 and 18 years old at Tenby, Wales.

Page 167

Me during my basic training in the RAF. I was based at Swinderby.

Chapter 21

Pages 172/173

Wendy and I on our Wedding Day and at our Wedding Breakfast.

Pages 175/176

Three brothers revisiting our old school East Brisbane State School where we had fond memories.

Page 177

Me in the back of the 10 seater 4x4 vehicle on Fraser Island.

Appendix 1

Pages 179/180/181

Formal photos of Fernley Manor.

Pages 182/183

Pages from the Fairsky Manifest regarding our accomdation at Yungaba.

Page 184

Me at a Maori settlement about age 15, from a day trip out.

Page 185

Walter at approximately age 30, well after we had settled back in the UK.

Page 186

Giles at approximately 13 years old when we lived in New Zealand.

Page 187

A school photo from when I was about 14. Walter and I are both on the back row. Walter 4th from the left and me, 4th from the right.

Page 187

Me ringing Wendy for a date. Our first date was at the Slow Boat Chinese Restaurant in Sleaford.

ACKNOWEDGEMENTS

I would like to thank everyone for helping with this book. In particular my wife Wendy, who encouraged me to keep writing and telling my story. For her help in proof reading the text and pointing out things which needed changing. She gave me the space to write and tell my story.

Also, grateful thanks to my publishers, Ladey Adey and Abbirose Adey. They gave me massive help and encouragement and spent a lot of hours guiding me through the process of writing. In the last year and a half particularly, their support was invaluable and I couldn't have achieved it without their help.

Thanks to my wider family, my children who encouraged me to keep writing and put up with my stories about tin cans for showers and a canoe for a bath and the various characters in the book. And lastly, to my friends who supported me through this process.

REFERENCES

Books

Landon, Joseph, & Kegan, Paul, *School Management*, (Trench, Truber & Co.), 1887

Websites

Delanie, Bernie, *Corporal Punishment Register*, (Facebook), https://www.facebook.com/photo/?fbid=841333382637415&set=a.270307679739991, 25/11/2022

Editorial Team, *Fremantle Passenger Terminal - Celebrating 50 years of arrivals and departures on Victoria Quay*, (Fremantle Ports), fremantle-passenger-terminal-50-years-anniversary-booklet.pdf (fremantleports.com.au), 30/12/2022

Editorial Team, *Admission Register - Victoria Point State School*, Queensland Government, (Queensland Government), https://www.archivessearch.qld.gov.au/items/ITM867307, 22/11/2022

Editorial Team, *Corporal punishment of children in Australia*, End Violence Against Children, (End Violence Against Children), https://www.endcorporalpunishment.org/wp-content/uploads/country-reports/Australia.pdf, 24/11/2022

Editorial Team, *Corporal punishment and health*, World Health Organisation, (World Health Organisation), https://www.who.int/news-room/fact-sheets/detail/corporal-punishment-and-health, 04/12/2022

Editorial Team, *Corporal punishment*, Queensland Government, (Queensland Government), https://education.qld.gov.au/about-us/history/history-topics/corporal-punishment, 25/11/2022

Editorial Team, *Corporal punishment still has support in Queensland*, School Governance, (Complispace), https://www.schoolgovernance.net.au/news/2014/08/15/corporal-punishment-still-has-support-in-queensland, 25/11/2022

Editorial Team, *Physical punishment legislation*, Australian Institute of Family Studies, (Australian Government), https://aifs.gov.au/resources/resource-sheets/physical-punishment-legislation#:~:text=Physical%20punishment%20was%20banned%20in,that%20it%20applies%20to%20both., 24/11/2022

Editorial Team, *Fairsky*, Ships Nostalgia, https://www.shipsnostalgia.com/media/fair-sky.250159/ 20/10/23

Editorial Team, *1968 flu pandemic*, Britannica, (Britannica), https://www.britannica.com/event/1968-flu-pandemic, 23/01/2023

Matthews, Alice, *In 2017, corporal punishment still legal in QLD non-government schools*, ABC News, (Australian Broadcasting Company), https://www.abc.net.au/triplej/programs/hack/corporal-punishment-qld/8310160, 25/11/2022

Miller, Rhea & Shea, George Beverly, *I'd Rather Have Jesus*, God Tube, (GodTube), https://www.godtube.com/popular-hymns/i-d-rather-have-jesus/ 15/09/2023

Unknown, *Immigration Camps*, Brisbane Immigration Camps, (Facebook), https://www.facebook.com/groups/10426022700/search/?q=immigration%20camps%20brisbane, 02/01/2023

Wikipedia Contributors, *Fairsky*, (Wikipedia), https://en.wikipedia.org/wiki/Fairsky, 07/03/2022

Wikipedia Contributors, *Yungaba Immigration Centre*, (Wikipedia), https://en.wikipedia.org/wiki/Yungaba_Immigration_Centre 20/10/23

Film

Metro-Goldwyn-Mayer, *Ben Hur*, Directed by William Wyler, (MGM), Santa Monica, CA, 1959

Paramount Pictures, *The Fall of the Roman Empire*, Directed by Anthony Mann, (Samuel Bronston Productions), Las Rozas, Spain, 1964

Music

Presley, Elvis, *Jailhouse Rock*, RCA Victor, (Jeff Alexander), Record, 1957, Album: Jailhouse Rock,

Seeger, Pete, *Little Boxes*, Columbia, Record, 1963

Various, *Molly Malone*, (James Yorkston), Trad Folk Song, circa 1884

Various, *Bobby Shaftoe*, (Unknown), Trad Folk Song, Circa 1737

ABOUT THE AUTHOR

Bob Oldershaw was born in Maidenhead. He has travelled extensively and lived in several countries. He now lives in Sleaford, Lincolnshire with his wife Wendy. This is his first book.

In his spare time he enjoys calligraphy and writing. He has three children, Daniel, Jonathan and Miriam who are all happily married. He has three beautiful grandchildren, Harriet, Lucy and Albie.

Bob served in the Royal Air Force for 22 years as a Communications Analyst. He is a church leader in a vibrant local church. He is involved in a number of volunteer roles including helping out at a Community Grocers and Chaplain to the Police. He is also a district Councillor providing help and support to the local community.

INDEX

A

Advance Australia Fair 77, 78
Alcott, Louisa May 67
Armstrong, Neil 120
Assisted Passage Migration Scheme 31
Astor, Lady Nancy 16

B

Banbury Baptist Church 164
Banbury Technical College 164
Bay of Biscay 6, 42
Beach Boys, The 98
Beatles, The 98, 120
Belfast 39
Ben Hur 68
Blackpool 11, 21
Bobby Shaftoe 29
Burke, Robert O'Hara 77

C

Calwell, Arthur 31
Cape Town 34
Cash, Johnny 120
Central St Martin's 167
Charing Cross Station 13
Chesterton, Gilbert Keith 14, 15, 18,
    19
Chifley, Benjamin 31
Christian Community Ministries Ltd
    (CCM) 88
Christie, Agatha 167
Churchill, Winston 75
Cook Islands 131
Corbett, Alan 88
Corporal punishment 73, 85, 86, 87,
    88
Curaçao 156

D

Dickens, Charles 67
    David Copperfield 40
    Oliver Twist 73
Dr Strangelove 110
Dylan, Bob 120

E

Enstone 160, 163, 167
Eyre, Edward John 77

F

Fernley 11, 14, 15, 17, 20
Fremantle 9, 37

G

Gauguin, Paul 155
Google 62
Gran Canaria
  Las Palmas 34
Great Australian Bight 9
Great Australian Bite 37

H

Hāngī 135, 136
Hong Kong Flu 122
Housman, A. E 40

I

Immigration Camps
  Comslie Immigration Centre 45
  Stuart Camp 45
  Wacol Hostel 45
  Yungaba Immigration Centre 45

K

Kennedy, John F 58

L

Larchfield Primary School 27
Lenin, Vladimir 154
London 12, 39
Lynn, Vera 98

M

Mackenzie, Scott 120
Maidenhead 3, 9, 15, 23, 24, 25, 28
Mediterranean Sea 6
Melbourne 9, 37
Miller, Rhea F 130
Molly Malone 29
MS Shota Rustaveli 153
Mullen, Willie 135

N

New South Wales 6
  Sydney 9, 34, 37, 39, 109, 110
New Zealand
  Arapohue Bush Camp 132, 134, 136,
    137, 168
  Auckland 38, 109, 110, 114, 121,
    129, 134, 137, 139, 143, 144
  Auckland Harbour 147, 149, 153
  Dargaville 129, 130, 131, 135, 138
  Devonport 110, 112, 114, 116, 117,
    125, 129, 139, 144, 147
  Greenhithe 117, 120, 121, 122,
    123, 135
    Takapuna Grammar 117
    Westlake Boy's High School 117
  Milford 117
  New Zealand School Certificate 119
  North Island 139, 147
    Lake Taupo 139, 143
    Napier 139, 140, 143
    North Head 114, 153
    Riverbend Christian Youth Camp
      141, 143
    Rotorua 148
  Nissan Huts 43, 44
  Northern Territory
    Darwin 178

O

O'Halloran Point 60
Oxford University 14, 17

P

Panama Canal 156
Poe, Edgar Alan 62
Poland 42
Port of Aden 6, 8, 37
Presley, Elvis 98, 99
Profumo, John 58

Q

Queensland 38, 51, 85, 86, 88
  Brisbane 3, 9, 38, 43, 44, 47, 48, 49,
    51, 59, 66, 67, 68, 69, 74, 90,
    99, 109, 174
    East Brisbane State School 47, 48,
      74, 174
  Cairns 178
  Cleveland 52, 55, 104, 174, 176
    Cleveland Yacht Club 104

Coochiemudlo 52, 53, 54, 55, 66, 175
Fraser Island 177
Gold Coast 99
Great Barrier Reef 178
Kuranda 178
Macleay Island 54
Mooggurapum Creek 56, 99
Noosa 176
O'Halloran Point 56, 59, 60, 63, 64, 65, 79, 81, 82, 84, 89, 93, 175
Redlands 62
Stradbroke Island 54
Surfer's Paradise 99
Victoria Point 51, 52, 53, 55, 56, 57, 58, 71, 72, 74, 81, 90, 93, 104, 174, 176
  Link Road 90, 93, 94, 95, 97, 99, 100, 101, 102, 103, 109
  Victoria Point State School 71, 72, 74, 176

R

Reader's Digest 67, 90
Rolling Stones, The 120
Rolls Royce 17, 163
Royal Air Force 165
Rupert Bear 29

S

Shadowlands 167
Shakespeare, William 13, 67
Shea, George Berverly 130
Shute, Neville 40
Sitmar 3, 33, 34, 110
  Castel Felice 32, 33, 34, 110
  Fairsea 32, 33, 34
  Fairsky 3, 32, 33, 34, 36, 37, 39, 110
    HMS Attacker 32
    Steel Artisan 32
Southampton 3, 34, 157, 158
South Australia
  Adelaide 9, 38
Southport 39

Spencer, Stanley 15, 82
SS Akorua 157
Stalin, Joseph 154
Stevenson, Robert Louis 40
St John Ambulance 121
St Pauls' School 17
Strait of Gibraltar 6
Suez Canal 6, 34, 37

T

Table Mountain 34
Tahiti 153, 154, 155
  Papeete 155
Taplow 23
The Fall of the Roman Empire 68
The Suggestive Handbook of Practical School Method 87

V

Vegemite 76
Victoria
  Melbourne 9, 37
Victoria Point State School 79

W

Waltzing Matilda 62
Ward, Stephen 58
Waterloo 41, 66, 159
Western Australia 32, 37
  Coolgardie 77
  Kalgoorlie 77
Wills, William John 77
Woodstock 120
Woolworths 164

NOTES

Please write any notes or questions you may have about my experiences as Ten Pound Pom. If you have any similar tales to tell, I would love to have a conversation about them with you - who knows we may even have lived in the same places or travelled on the same ship!

Milton Keynes UK
Ingram Content Group UK Ltd.
UKHW020444221223
434798UK00001B/1

9 781913 579685